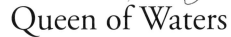

Queen of Waters

A Journey in Time along the Kennet & Avon Canal

This book is dedicated to all those people who, in their many and various ways,
worked to restore the Kennet & Avon Canal,
but, above all, to
JOHN GOULD
8 June 1913 – 19 March 1999
without whom there would be no Kennet & Avon Canal today.

Queen of Waters

A Journey in Time along the Kennet & Avon Canal

Kirsten Elliott

AKEMAN
PRESS

Published by Akeman Press, 58 Minster Way, Bath BA2 6RL
www.akemanpress.com

ISBN   978-0-9560989-2-4

Front cover & half title page: The Canal in Sydney Gardens, Bath, from a pastel by Nick Cudworth.

Back cover, clockwise from top left: *Kennet Valley* in Dreweatt's Lock, May 1972; Widcombe Carnival, September 1974; Kintbury Lock in the 1890s; A Toast to the Queen of Waters; Caen Hill Flight, Devizes, May 1971; Heading East out of Bruce Tunnel.

Page 200: The Canal in Sydney Gardens, Bath in 1890.

Page 202: 'Queen of Waters' from the CD *Twice Reflected Sun* by Nancy Kerr & James Fagan, produced by Navigator Records (NAVIGATOR041).

Page 203: At Wilcot, c1905.

Printed by Butler Tanner & Dennis Ltd, Frome, Somerset

Contents

Foreword

It is 200 years since the opening of the Kennet & Avon Canal. This remarkable and enduring feat of human endeavour was our home from 1999 until 2010. How lucky we have been to experience its every season; mists curling on autumn mornings, thick winter freezes, May blossoms, and the splendid ease of summer living. We met the canal through seasoned live-aboard friends and first explored its stretches among the chalk hills and white horses east of Devizes. Since then we've travelled its length aboard our three narrowboat homes, as well as putting down roots (well, ropes) for several years in the village of Bathampton. As an Australian, James was amazed to discover, just metres from the canal at Bathampton, the final resting place of Captain Arthur Phillip, who led the First Fleet to establish Sydney Town in 1788 – the same year that Charles Dundas began the campaign for a Western Canal.

A measure of our love for the K&A was our impulsive decision in June 2007 to take our boat from Bathampton up the famous lock flight at Caen Hill to Honeystreet for our honeymoon. Some might see such an undertaking as more hard work than romance, but imagine a shining new boat ascending the flight on a summer's day, bedecked with wedding flowers and ribbons, filled to the gunwales with champagne, hampers of edible wedding presents and a leftover barrel of Brassknocker Ale. We had no trouble finding volunteers to help us with all those locks, and when we arrived at the Barge Inn at Honeystreet we drank down the sun overlooking the White Horse as the swans and moorhens bobbed around us on the tranquil pink water, and were so glad we hadn't gone to Paris.

For boaters, as for many who today travel and live with less space and fewer comforts, small daily achievements engender a sense of triumph as they must have in 1810 – collecting fuel, getting the stove lit, cooking and washing and generally staying afloat. Some moments are pure magic. One September evening just west of Newbury, towards the end of a long cruise from the Midlands, we pulled up at a rural lock, tired and hoping for a pub meal, to find that the pound ahead had accidentally been completely drained. We gazed at the muddy V-shaped expanse. Birdsong seemed amplified by the emptiness, and the light was somehow wrong. Stranded for the night, we fashioned a miraculous dinner from our meagre stores – baked potatoes, lentils and a bottle of merlot. We still remember it as a legendary meal.

Seeing the canal waterless that evening, we had a rare sense of its hand-dug yet sleekly engineered shape. You get to know each lock's character and quirks, the feel of certain patches of water by the way your tiller snags and catches. There's a leap of faith that the boat will go round that bend, through that bridge hole, turn at that winding point, moor near that bank. It works, for the most part, like a well-evolved organism.

We've always felt that the world of the inland waterways is a different realm, at once magical and real. As folk musicians, singing an old song or playing a traditional tune opens a similar window onto the evolving history of ordinary people. We perceive the music as it was decades ago, we feel ourselves shaping it now, and we guess at where it might go in the hands of generations to come. Kirsten's book paints for us the details, colours and characters that form the extraordinary story of the K&A Canal, a story that will always be part of our lives.

Nancy Kerr and James Fagan, September 2010

Introduction

I cannot remember when or in which book I first read about the Kennet & Avon Canal, but I know that whichever book it was, the great flight of locks at Devizes was mentioned. For some reason, the idea of it appealed to my imagination. So when we came to live in Bath, in 1960, I persuaded my parents to take me out to see it. I can still remember my dismay at finding this wonder of engineering in what appeared to be terminal decay.

However, living in Bath, I came to know the Widcombe flight well, and made friends with people who were involved in trying to make at least a stretch of canal workable. They helped out on boats such as the *Charlotte Dundas*, designed by Lt-Cmdr Wray-Bliss to chew up the choking duckweed, while giving pleasure trips to visitors. But could these efforts ever really see the canal reopened?

It was in those heady days of the Sixties, when, looking back, summer days all seemed halcyon, I discovered the pleasure of walking with my dog from Dundas Basin into Bath along the towpath. In those days, there were just pools of water in the aqueduct, and a pair of sometimes aggressive swans had made their home in the reed-infested basin. They took strong exception to a black miniature poodle intruding on their quiet, secure haven. The towpath then was a narrow strip between grassy banks studded with wild flowers. Dragonflies zoomed across the still waters of the canal; birds fluttered in the reeds on one side of the path or the hedges on the other, surprised by our presence. We

Left: Caen Hill Flight, Devizes, May 1971.

would rarely see another person until we neared Sydney Gardens. In many ways it was an idyllic, secret world – but it was not what the canal was intended for. It was a picturesque and ornamental dereliction, but it was dereliction all the same.

Despite the dereliction, the canal could be a lively place. It certainly was in the bitter winter of 1962-3, when the normally quiet stretch between Bathwick Hill and the Widcombe flight rang with the hiss of skates, the chatter of onlookers, and the sound of laughter. Even those who weren't up to skating took the rare opportunity of walking on its frozen surface.

I left Bath in 1968 but returned in 1981, and immediately joined the K&A Canal Trust. I was impressed by the progress of restoration. Back in the Sixties it had seemed an impossible dream. In their heart of hearts, even some of those idealists who talked about the canal reopening, and who expended great efforts in trying to achieve that goal, never really thought it would happen. But now, suddenly, it looked as though the dream might be coming true. There was talk of reopening the whole canal by 1983.

But when in 1982 I walked it, all the way from Reading to Hanham, it was evident that there was much left to do. Many locks, especially at the eastern end, were still ruinous, the gates, rotten and decayed, hanging from their hinges. In some places, they had simply collapsed into the lock. Devizes remained a problem – as it had been when the canal was first built. Landslips, leaks and water shortages, not to mention a lorry crashing into a bridge at Bath were all backward steps in the progress of restoration. Chatting with volunteers at Crofton Pumping Station, it was clear that, despite the brave words, there was a certain amount of pessimism. It was not until 1990 that the Queen finally declared the Kennet & Avon Canal open once more.

In the 20 years since then, the Kennet & Avon Canal has changed beyond recognition, from that dreaming backwater into a well-used waterway which has brought new industry to places such as Hilperton and Aldermaston. It is a leisure facility enjoyed by many – not just boaters and anglers but walkers and cyclists as well. Its once quiet towpath is now part of a busy cycle route which allows the fit and adventurous to cross the country on two wheels. It has also become a home to many who cannot afford to buy a house in expensive Bath and choose to live afloat instead. It is a testament to all those, including myself, who kept faith with the idea that it could be done, and who contributed our many and varied talents to achieving the aim. Two hundred years ago, in December 1810, the canal was – finally – completely open. Against all the odds, it is open once again.

This book is a celebration not only of the 200th anniversary of the opening of the canal, but also the 20th anniversary of its reopening. In it we take a journey along the canal from Reading on the River Thames to Bristol on the River Avon – a journey in time, with pictures and photographs showing the changes that have occurred over the past two centuries.

Although I have split the walk into five quite lengthy sections – six if you include the stretch to Bristol – I do not suggest that you try to tackle these as a complete section each day. I have just done this because the canal falls into five logical sections. In Appendix 2, I give a table of mileages along the canal to help you judge convenient distances to walk.

The book also gives some guidance on walking the towpath, with a few helpful hints on where to stay and where to find refreshment. It is not just intended for those familiar with canals but for those to whom they are a new experience. For them, I have included a short section at the end (Appendix 1) in which I answer some frequently asked questions.

Above all, the book is an expression of the pleasure I have had over the years in discovering the towns, the people, and the scenery along the Kennet & Avon Canal – a pleasure which I am happy to share with others.

Kirsten Elliott, Bath, September 2010

Right: Bath Narrowboats wharf.

1 A Brief History

A journey is always more rewarding if you know something of the history of the places you are to visit. For those who want an exhaustive history of the canal, Kenneth Clew's book, *The Kennet & Avon Canal*, first published in 1968, and revised in 1973, remains the most thorough work. It is not, however, an easy read. A much more approachable history, by Warren Berry, Curator of the Kennet & Avon Canal Trust Museum in Devizes, was published in 2009, bringing the story up to date. This chapter in no way sets out to compete with either of those books. It is intended as a brief history to give you a broad picture of what you will be looking at as you travel along the canal. More detailed history will be given at the relevant points in later chapters.

The idea of a waterway linking Bristol with London had been around for a very long time. Anyone wishing to ship goods across the country had either to entrust their merchandise to jolting carts or pack animals on the deplorable roads or risk a dangerous journey around Land's End and up the English Channel. In addition to storms, shipwrecks and other maritime dangers, England was frequently at war with its European neighbours, who regarded loaded merchant ships as legitimate prizes. Even those who did not envisage a cross-country route were demanding that the Bristol Avon be made navigable as far upstream as possible.

For a variety of reasons, all these schemes came to nothing. About 1626, Henry Briggs of Merton College, Oxford pointed out that the headwaters of the Avon and the Thames were only about three miles apart near Malmesbury in Wiltshire. It would not take much effort to unite them. Briggs' early death and the advent of the Civil War silenced these ideas for a while, but a friend of Briggs called Francis Mathew revived the scheme. After the restoration of the monarchy in 1660, several attempts were made to push this and similar ideas through parliament, but all to no avail.

Similar fates befell the various schemes to make the Avon navigable as far as Bath, despite a plaintive plea from Bath Corporation that it was needed because road transport from Bristol was difficult and expensive 'by reason of rockie and mountaynous waies'. The opposition to all these schemes was just too strong.

Above: The Lower Bristol Road, Bath about 1800, showing pack animals, their saddles heaped high with goods, struggling along the rutted road, while a coach comes the other way. On the left, the sail of a boat on the Avon Navigation can be seen in the distance.

Opposite: The restoration of the canal in the late 1970s and 1980s revived scenes that would have familiar to the navigators who built it almost two centuries earlier. This photograph was taken near Avoncliff in December 1976.

It may seem odd that there was opposition to these plans, given that Wiltshire and Berkshire had no coal, whereas Gloucestershire and Somerset were well-supplied with it. Bristol was also an important port where highly desirable goods were imported into the country. But that was part of the problem. There were too many powerful people with vested interests in maintaining the status quo, especially landowners and farmers. The last thing they wanted was to see cheap imported goods driving down prices. Even mine owners in the Somerset coalfield were against it, fearing the import of Shropshire coal, apparently lacking the vision to see that it could be used to export their coal to the neighbouring coal-starved counties.

Another source of opposition was mill-owners. There were many kinds of mill on the Avon – some for grinding corn, others, known locally as tucking mills, for fulling cloth. The millers certainly had no wish to see the river made navigable, in case it reduced the flow to their waterwheels. So, although an act was passed in 1712 to make the Avon navigable as far as Bath, nothing happened. Goods continued to be bumped along in lumbering carts or on the backs of pack animals.

It was a group of people in Reading who seized the initiative. It was not, as it turned out, a popular move with many in Reading. Reading's history as an inland port begins with the monks of Reading Abbey. They created wharfs on the River Kennet and its tributary, the Holy Brook. Even after the dissolution of the monasteries in 1539, Reading continued to be a bustling, industrial town. After the wool trade – its first main source of income – declined, other industries took its place. Pin, wire and nail making were all established by the early seventeenth century. Gun Street is named after the gunsmiths. One of the most important industries was brick and tile making and there was also a large corn market. The last thing many traders in Reading wanted was change.

But others had been casting envious eyes on Reading's prosperity. Newbury's townsfolk, further upstream on the Kennet, saw no reason why some of this wealth should not come to them, and towns as far afield as Trowbridge and Bradford on Avon in Wiltshire supported them. By 1715, an Act of Parliament had been passed to allow the Kennet to be made navigable, despite the protests of Reading. However, three years passed, and the merchants of Reading must have been about to breathe a sigh of relief. The first engineers were incompetent, and hardly anything had been achieved. Work had to be completed by 1721 and time was running out.

The company decided to call in John Hore of Newbury; they also managed to get a two-year extension to the deadline. Hore realised the easiest way was to canalise the most meandering sections of the river; eventually, of the 18½ miles of the navigation, only seven were actually along

This early photograph of a turf-sided lock shows how they appeared by the mid-nineteenth century, after they were widened to take Newbury barges. Today only Garston Lock, of which this may be a picture, gives any idea of what it was like to use such a lock.

the river. Locks were also required, and, with no water supply problems to worry about, Hore designed these with timber supports below the water and turf sides above, This meant that they were cheaper, and quicker to construct. The navigation opened within the time limit set for it.

Reading was outraged. Barge-owners received death threats, boats and their crews were pelted with mud, and at one point, in 1720, while work was still in progress, a mob, led by Robert Blake, Mayor of Reading, set out to destroy what had been achieved so far. Eventually, however, Reading realised that, far from robbing it of business, the navigation attracted more trade. Yet for a long time the Kennet Navigation did not flourish as it should. Matters improved when Lady Forbes, widow of one of the early proprietors, with a shrewd business brain, took a keen interest in the navigation. But its fortunes still fluctuated until the Page family took an active hand in its management from about 1760 onwards.

It is, perhaps, surprising that Bath lagged behind in making the River Avon navigable, but, as we have seen, there were many powerful voices raised against it. Eventually, however, they were outgunned when a consortium including the Duke of Beaufort, John Hobbs of Bristol, a wealthy deal merchant, and Ralph Allen took on the enterprise in 1724.

Allen is often thought of as a benign, kindly character, thanks partly to being associated with Fielding's Squire Allworthy in *Tom Jones*. It was an image that he was probably happy to foster. Tigers like people to think they are pussy-cats – it puts those who deal with them off their guard. And in reality Allen was a tiger, a ruthless operator, who, with the help of the architect John Wood, broke the power of the stonemasons in Bath, and who manipulated the political activities of Bath Corporation for years.

With men like these on board, the result was inevitable – in December 1727 the first cargoes arrived in Bath. The speed and economy with which the Avon Navigation had been built was partly due to the fact there was no horse-towing path – boats were man-hauled. It was not all plain sailing – in 1738, Saltford Lock was blown up and the culprits were widely thought to have been Somerset coal miners, since a threatening letter promised more such attacks if transporting coal by water did not cease. Eventually, matters settled down. The navigation, in fact, proved beneficial to the local collieries and a tramway was built from the South Gloucestershire coalfields to a wharf on the River Avon.

The Avon Navigation officially terminated upstream at the weir below Pulteney Bridge in Bath. Most boats, however, moored downstream of the Old Bridge, seen here in the late eighteenth century. A variety of craft can be seen, with goods stacked up on Broad Quay on the left.

A campaign for a Western Canal, using one or both of the navigations, began in 1788, when a group led by Charles Dundas, who lived at Kintbury, mooted the idea at a series of meetings. The 29-year old John Rennie was appointed engineer – a surprising choice, since at that time he had little experience of canals, but one that would link his name forever with this form of transport.

Over the next few years there were various proposals, but eventually, in April 1794, the Kennet & Avon Canal Act received Royal Assent. Four canals were proposed to link with it. Two – the Somersetshire Coal Canal and the Wilts & Berks Canal – were built, while one – the Dorset & Somerset Canal – was begun but not completed. Progress was slow and costs rose constantly. Rennie is often admired for his use of Bath stone, most notably in his aqueducts. In fact he had no wish to use it, preferring the more reliable brick, but many of the landowners were quarry-owners too, and this was to sweeten them and encourage them

Portrait of John Rennie, painted by Sir Henry Raeburn in 1810.

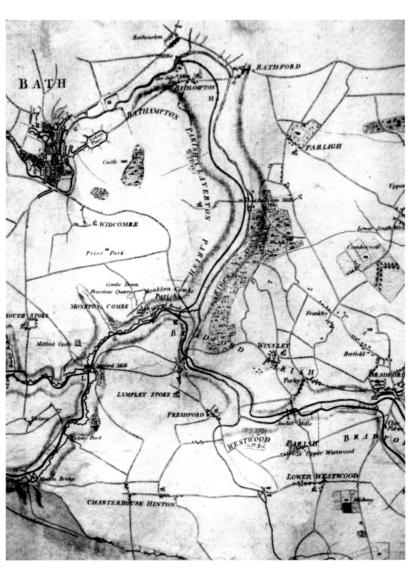

This map shows the original route planned into Bath, joining the River Avon at Bathampton. The Somersetshire Coal Canal, with its two branches – to Timsbury and Radstock – can be seen branching off the Kennet & Avon north of Limpley Stoke.

The planned Bath and Bristol canal, whose route through Bath is shown on this plan, was originally going to avoid Sydney Gardens. Instead of continuing the canal to Bristol, however, a cut down to the Avon at Widcombe – sketched in on this plan – was adopted.

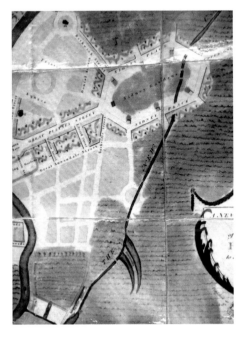

This plan shows the route finally adopted at Sydney Gardens, with the 'New Canal' cutting through the north-east end.

to be customers when the canal opened. Unfortunately, the stone was often of poor quality, and had to be replaced in locks, bridges and aqueducts. The canal bed also leaked and had to be relined. The cost of fencing rose. Mills had to be purchased to avoid annual charges for water rights. Costs of material and labour rose due to inflation caused by the Napoleonic Wars.

The middle section of the canal needed more lining than expected. Debts were outstanding to the Company. The geology caused problems in the Limpley Stoke Valley, seven acres subsiding as work began at Bradford on Avon. The first plan had been for the canal to join the River Avon at Bathampton, but then a Bath to Bristol Canal was proposed, avoiding the twists and turns of the Avon Navigation. Work proceeded, thus incurring expense at Bath when the proprietors of Sydney Gardens demanded 2,000 guineas to allow the canal through. They also demanded ornamental bridges 'in the manner of the Chinese'. It must have been very galling for the Canal Company to see the canal subsequently advertised as an attraction.

Nevertheless, the eastern and western ends slowly grew longer and began to look as though they might finally meet. As each section opened, it came into use so that when work began on the final obstacle, the great flight of locks at Caen Hill, a tramway was built down the towpath to enable goods to travel along the canal while the locks and their accompanying side-pounds were carved out of the hillside. The work was finally completed in December 1810, and on the 28th of that month a barge loaded with freestone ascended the flight. There were no celebrations. It had all taken so long and cost so much more than first thought. Before work had even started the projected cost rose by over £100,000 to £336,365, but the final cost was about £1 million.

Once open, however, it proved successful, paying reasonable dividends (about 2½ to 3%) to shareholders. Goods carried on it included building materials of various kinds, ashes (used for mortar), metals such as iron, tin, copper and brass, and foodstuffs such as fruit, sugar, tea, and biscuits. On one occasion a French packet carrying linen drapery came up from London, and travelled down the canal to Bristol. The most important cargo was coal, and it was undoubtedly the owners of the Somerset coalfields who were the most important customers of the Kennet & Avon. Without the short Somersetshire Coal Canal, which, despite its length, was one of the most successful canals on the entire waterway system, the K&A would have struggled. On the other hand, it was thanks to the canal that the coalfields flourished, with new markets open to them. For a time the waterways revolutionised transport. By and large, the canals carried goods rather than visitors, but passengers were not neglected. Craft such as the Scotch Boat, which ran from Bath to Bradford on Avon, provided a smooth, regular and surprisingly quick service. A string band was provided as entertainment.

However, it was not long before the writing was on the wall. Railways were evolving from the simple, horse-drawn tramways of the past into a more efficient and faster form of transport than had ever been seen before. At first, the canal companies dismissed the threat of the steam-powered locomotives that hauled trains on the new rail-roads. In 1824 a prospectus was published proposing a railway between London and Bristol, and Mr. Blackwell, the K&A Canal Company's engineer, was sent north 'to see the operation of several Rail Roads and Locomotive Engines now in work and to report his opinion and observations thereon'. He happily stated that 'there are limits to their powers, which are nearly approached.'

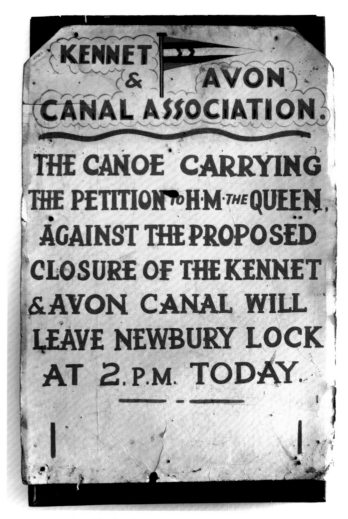

A poster printed by the K&A Trust in 1956 to advertise the departure of the canoe carrying the petition.

Less than twenty years later, the GWR line between Bristol and London opened. As the railway network spread, many canals were bought up by railway companies and converted to trackbeds – they had the advantage of being level. Locally, this was the case in 1903, when the GWR acquired the Somersetshire Coal Canal and turned it into the Camerton & Limpley Stoke Railway. However, although the GWR purchased the K&A in 1852, it remained a canal. The canal company had battled against the railway, undercutting its charges to the point where trade actually began to pick up. Unfortunately, due to the drastic reduction in tolls, income continued to drop, and eventually the K&ACC was forced to sell out to the GWR. It stipulated in the contract, however, that the railway company should maintain the canal and keep it navigable. Rather surprisingly the directors agreed to this, but after a time it became apparent that the intention was that the canal should quietly wither away. Traffic was not encouraged, and ice-breaking was stopped just before the winter of 1857, resulting in boats being frozen in. Tolls rose, and even pleasure boats were discouraged.

Eventually some traders, notably the Gerrish family, began to take the GWR to court, with some success, and two Acts of Parliament, in 1873 and 1888, stressed that where railway companies owned canals, it was in the public interest that they should maintain them. With the nationalisation of the railways, further efforts were made to close the canal, but it simply would not die. Pressure groups like the K&A Trust were formed, sometimes using surprising methods of protest. In January 1956, a petition carrying 20,000 signatures was addressed to the queen. It left Bristol on a cutter called *Foam* and then transferred to a canoe, which was paddled from Bath to Thames Ditton. Here, the canoe and its contents were transferred to a Maid

Appealing for volunteers: May 1971.

Line cruiser and taken to Westminster, where the Minister for Transport received it on behalf of Her Majesty.

At last, the establishment's opposition to saving the canal cracked and work began. After many years of effort, negotiations with councils, quangos, unions and other interested parties, the Kennet & Avon Trust's dream came true on 8th August 1990, when the Queen re-opened the canal. In 1994, a cargo of Bath stone once again travelled down the K&A on a narrowboat, 200 years after the whole project had begun.

2 Getting There: A Walkers', Cyclists' and Boaters' Guide

It might surprise some people to think that you need a guide to explore a canal. The obvious rule would seem to be: start at one end, keep going until you reach the other end, then stop. Sadly, life isn't as simple as that. Even walkers need to be alert to make sure that they are on the towpath and not a path made by anglers, which may end up being a dead end in the middle of a field. Boaters – as all experienced boaters know – need to check for stoppages, availability of moorings, restrictions on lock usage and so on. So here are a few tips for getting the best out of the canal.

You will notice this guide is not for motorists. That is because using your car is the least efficient way of visiting the Kennet & Avon. Parking is often restricted, and you may end up walking quite a distance before you even get to the canal. However, if you want to explore short sections, then Bradford on Avon, Devizes, and Hungerford all have large car parks close to the canal. All offer walks of variety, with scenic and historic points of interest, and all three towns are interesting to explore in their own right. There is also parking in Newbury at the old wharf, but this is expensive if you are planning to walk all day. As we will see, the canal is particularly well served by public transport, and if you want to explore short sections, then bus or rail is advised. See below, in the walkers' section, for details of this. There are, of course, attractions along the canal, such as Crofton Pumping Station, and many pubs, which have their own parking.

The first tip for all users is to visit a website called *www.waterscape.com*. It is run by British Waterways, and is invaluable for anyone wanting to explore Britain's waterways. It has descriptions of circular walks, maps, canal and towpath closures. For boaters, it lists useful information such as chandleries, marinas, moorings, and where you can pump out and take on water. It can, however, be somewhat optimistic – some of the pubs and restaurants that it lists along the K&A, for example, are a considerable distance from the canal.

Cyclists

Waterscape is very enthusiastic about cyclists using the Kennet & Avon towpath, but cycling is not the ideal way to discover the canal. At *www.waterscape.com/canals-and-rivers/kennet-and-avon-canal/cycling* you can download the map of the National Cycle Route. Although the route sticks fairly closely to the waterway, and the climbs are mainly gentle, a quick inspection shows quite long sections where the cycle route leaves the canal, as the towpath is described as unsuitable. If you have a mountain bike, then you would be able to press on, but most cyclists prefer to stick to the National Route, as the going can be difficult where the

under them. Not only will this save you from bumping your head, but the approaches along the path to nearly all the stone or brick-built bridges are such that pedestrians coming the other way do not see you until the last moment. If you swoop under a bridge without giving any warning, you may meet walkers coming the other way at a point where your only option to avoid a collision will be to go into the canal.

Between Kintbury and Newbury, you may come across the Kennet Horse Boat Company's barge, *Kennet Valley*. The horses which pull this are gentle and friendly, but they are quite large and take up a lot of path. At least stop to let them go by. And, of course, they do leave their calling cards on the towpath, so if you see the horse, you know what else to watch out for.

Finally, an unwanted hazard is motorcyclists. They are not supposed to be on the towpath – a fact of which they are well aware – but particularly near Burghfield there are occasionally some young men who find it entertaining to ride up and down the path at high speed. This is bad enough for walkers, but at least walkers can jump out of the way. Cyclists are more at risk, so listen out for the sound of trail bikes and be aware that they may be coming in your direction.

Wheelchair Users

The Waterscape website is sadly lacking in information for wheelchair users, which is a pity as some sections of the towpath are ideal for wheelchairs. The National Cycle Route map can offer some guidance, however. Where the route leaves the canal, then the going for wheelchairs will also be difficult, and the map gives possible routes round obstructions.

There are some additional hazards. At Bath, for example, where you might expect wheelchair-friendly access, the road crossing at Bathwick Hill presents you with steps on one side,

path goes through fields. This means that cyclists miss some picturesque parts of the canal. The same web page also offers some short cycle rides, with details of public transport – for more details of rail transport, see the walkers' section, below.

Cyclists should watch out for walkers – please ring your bell if you are approaching from behind, and remember many people may have small children and dogs with them. Where the path is wide and in good condition, there may also be wheelchair users – in fact, with the advent of trail wheelchairs, you may even come across them where you might not be expecting them. Anglers frequently leave gear on the towpath, or may lift their rods over the path. Most mooring ropes are clear of the towpath, but again, there may be clutter on the path as you pass boats where people are living – and many people now live along the canal. So you need to have your wits about you.

On some occasions you may have to get off and walk. Near Woolhampton there is a stretch of the path which is in private hands, and the owners insist that cyclists dismount. Many of the bridges are low, and you should get off to go and a steep ramp with pitched setts – giving a very bumpy ride – on the other. The only way round this, if heading east, is to avoid the canal from Widcombe and gain access from Beckford Road, north of Sydney Gardens. After that, you are on the wide section which runs all the way to Devizes. Your only hazards then are the long climb at Caen Hill, some steep climbs to roving bridges – where the towpath crosses from one side to the other – and narrow sections of the path under bridges, which take the chair's wheels worryingly close to the edge.

Another wide section runs from Reading to Marsh Benham, including a pleasant canalside walk through Newbury. These two wide sections were developed with help from Sustrans for cyclists, and the path is fairly even, giving a comfortable ride. Some of the footbridges, however, although ramped, are quite long and steep. You need to check your access points. Most bridges carrying footpaths and roads give pedestrian access, but many are unsuitable for wheelchairs, and in some cases, even for pushchairs with small children. For standard wheelchairs, other sections are far more problematic, with the path going through fields or narrowing to the width of a normal footpath. For those with trail wheelchairs, who are determined to see as much of the canal as possible, perhaps the best course of action is to visit the Kennet & Avon Canal Trust website, *www.katrust.org*, which gives contact details for the seven local branches which can give detailed advice on accessibility.

Boaters

Seeing the K&A from a boat is perhaps the most enjoyable way of travelling, and, if you've never done it before, will bring you closer to understanding the way of life along the canal. As the canal can take boats up to 12 feet (3.7m) wide (14 feet (4.3m) between Reading and Newbury), you will find barges as well as narrowboats, including some picturesque Dutch barges.

There are many ways of enjoying a waterborne journey on the canal. There are several trip boats, some run by the Kennet & Avon Canal Trust and others by commercial marinas. The Kennet Horse Boat Company says that you can 'choose between the slow meandering of the motor barge and the sedate drifting of the horse-drawn barge'. If you have never travelled on a horse-drawn boat, this is an experience not to be missed. The gentle footfall of the horse along the path and the ripple of the water beneath the bow are the only sounds to be heard, and make us realise how noisy our modern world is by comparison with the past.

This and other companies offer day boat hire for those wishing to get the feel of doing it themselves on the canal before embarking on a full holiday. However, remember there is a speed limit of 4mph on the canal– your hirer will not thank you if he is bombarded with irate phone calls from anglers and other boaters if you ignore the limit.

Canoeing is another option, but unless you are a member of the BCU you will need a licence (as all boat owners do). There are many canoe clubs along the canal,

and canoes can be hired from the Bath & Dundas Canal Company, at Brassknocker Basin.

Those planning a trip in a boat will find a guide to the canal on the Kennet & Avon pages of the Waterscape website, but, although it is smartly presented, there is a more detailed boaters' guide on the same website, which is regularly updated. It has information on everything you need to know, from services and facilities, stoppages, moorings and maps to navigational guidance. Because the canal incorporates two river navigations, there are often currents, some of them quite fierce when you are near a weir – the guide advises you on these. However, you will not find it under the Kennet & Avon pages, but under Boaters' Guides on the home page.

However, if you are prepared to spend a few pounds, there is a much better guide available. Without doubt, the best guide for boaters is by Niall Allsop, who once lived on a narrowboat on the canal. Called *The Kennet & Avon Canal – A User's Guide*, it was last published in 1999, so some of the information is out of date, but by and large it is invaluable. It can be obtained from Millstream Books of Bath.

Moorings may well be an issue during busy summer periods. At the end of a long summer's day, you may find yourself having to moor some distance from a village pub, so you should be well-stocked up with food and drink. Mooring in the centre of Reading may be hazardous – some boaters have woken up to find that they have been quietly cast adrift overnight. This does not seem to happen in Bath, but if you are nervous, there are secure moorings at the Bath Marina on the River Avon. This marina also has laundry facilities.

Although a canal holiday is in many ways very restful, parts of it can be hard work. Regular boaters know that shifting swing bridges can be heavy going – some boat owners even carry a crowbar. On one stretch between Seend and Semington, where there are a lot of swing bridges, it is easier for a crew member to swing the bridges and walk on to the next one rather than keep climbing aboard. Flights of locks need teamwork if you are going to negotiate them without long delays. So at least some of your crew need to be fit.

Some locks are notorious. Widcombe Deep Lock needs care, especially when descending. People have come to grief when the back of the boat has stuck on the cill of the lock and no one has noticed until the boat was already tipping alarmingly. Hungerford Marsh Lock has a swing bridge passing over it, which needs to be swung out of the way first – unless you want to decapitate your steersman. Then there is the flight of locks at Caen Hill – 16 close together and 29 spread over two miles. As the balance beams are all at different heights, your crew will find that after tackling this, they will probably ache from their shoulders down to their knees, but they should also have a sense of achievement at having worked their way up one of the seven wonders of the waterways (according to Robert Aickman, co-founder of the Inland Waterways Association).

Boats can be hired at various places along the canal. Beginners should be given full instruction by hirers before setting out – if you are not confident, don't be afraid to ask questions. The Bruce Trust has four boats which are specially adapted so that the disabled, disadvantaged and elderly can also enjoy a self-catering holiday afloat. And here's one final tip to those new to waterways. As all regular boaters will know, you should always have more than one windlass. That's the giant spanner you need for opening the paddles at locks. You will look very silly if you lose your only windlass overboard.

And finally … walkers

This is the way most people are going to explore the Kennet & Avon Canal, whether they take it in short stretches or walk the full 87 miles. Although it does not have the same atmosphere as travelling along in a boat, it does allow you – provided you haven't set yourself impossible schedules – to stop and talk to the many people you will meet as you travel along.

If you just want to tackle short stretches, then where the canal passes through Wiltshire you may be able to use the Connect2Wiltshire bus service to get you to your starting point. Call 08456 525255 to book a place, having first checked the number of the bus stop where you want to board. For people walking either end of the canal, there are rail services covering the sections from Keynsham to Trowbridge, and from Reading to Pewsey.

If walking it in one go, you can carry everything and simply walk, stopping along the way overnight – although you will need to plan your stops carefully. However, one easy way, which means you don't need to carry so much, is to use two centres. I would recommend Hungerford and Bath. There are regular train services between Reading and Hungerford, stopping at Theale, Aldermaston, Midgham (for Woolhampton), Thatcham, Newbury and Kintbury. In the other direction, the train runs from Hungerford to

Bedwyn. To reach or return from Pewsey, you will need to go to Newbury and change. Between Pewsey and Devizes there is no train service. However, a regular bus service, First bus 271/272/273, runs every hour between Devizes and Bath. Once based at Bath, it's back to the train, with stations at Trowbridge, Bradford on Avon, Avoncliff (a request stop) and Freshford to the east of Bath, and Oldfield Park and Keynsham to the west. If ending your walk along the canal at Hanham, the western end, you will have to walk back to Keynsham Station to pick up the train, unless you plan to walk on into Bristol along the Avon Walkway.

Before setting out, you could also consider whether you really want to walk the whole canal. Remember, it does not finish at Bath – the Avon Walkway continues to Hanham, with Bristol another six miles further on. If you are interested in industrial history, or if you simply want the pleasure of saying you've walked the whole 87 miles from Reading to Hanham, then do it, but be aware that not all of it is beautiful countryside. Reading itself is an interesting town, but the canal runs past some uninspired modern architecture,

through a busy modern shopping centre and under flyovers and motorways. Being a canal, it served industry, and some industrial buildings still border it. If a peaceful walk through delightful scenery is what you are after, then you might prefer to start (assuming you are travelling east to west) at Theale, and end at Bath. That is not to say that parts of the River Avon walk are not lovely – they are – but having joined the River Avon at Bath, you are faced with a walk past such delights as Homebase, the council tip, an industrial estate and the site of the old gasworks before you reach open fields again. From Theale to Bath is a walk of nearly 70 miles, so still quite an achievement if you haven't walked long distances before.

If it is your first attempt at long-distance walking, make sure you have comfortable footwear. Proper walking boots or shoes are not a luxury but a necessity if you are walking far, especially if you are doing it day after day. Have sticking plasters to give quick attention to any blisters. If the weather is hot, take sun protection cream – if it's changeable, make sure you have some reliable waterproof clothing and a waterproof rucksack.

Even though following the canal should be straight-forward, you will need maps if you are going to make diversions from the canal, and to find out where the stations are. There are new walkway routes on the River Avon, and these are marked on the latest Ordnance Survey maps. If you can get your hands on copies of Nicholas Hammond's two Kennet & Avon Waterway maps, first published in 1969 and 1975, you will find that his detailed charts mean you can work out exactly where you are, how fast you are walking – the route is measured in miles and chains – and what the next feature, such as a bridge or aqueduct, is. It shows when the towpath changes sides, which is where you can come to grief if you follow the wrong path. Even though they are out of date, since new bridges have been added, they are still invaluable companions to have on your walk. It would be nice to think that updated versions will one day be published.

Finally, whatever you do, take your time. It is strange and rather sad that people should congratulate themselves on walking the canal as quickly as possible. They must be

A timeless scene: near Bathampton, April 1990

missing so much. The pace of life along a canal is slow. Allow time to chat with people. Watch the flora and fauna. Notice how the landscape changes as you travel. Your enjoyment of the journey will be enhanced if you spend time exploring some of the canalside towns, or attractions such as the pumping stations at Crofton and Claverton, if they are open. There are some very good pubs by or near the canal, some serving excellent food.

With those thoughts, let us now begin a journey in time along this Queen of Waters, the Kennet & Avon Canal.

3 Reading to Newbury: The Kennet Navigation

Archaeologists have shown that the Thames has had permanent settlements beside it since Neolithic times. It has been used as a means of invasion, but also as a form of defence. It provided power for industry, irrigation for crops, even food thanks to its fish. It has been used for pleasure: as a desirable backdrop to places built by the rich and powerful or for Victorian young men, like those in *Three Men in a Boat*, to show off their prowess as oarsmen. But above all, it was, like the River Severn in the west, used for trade.

The Kennet & Avon Canal was built to link these two great waterways, without the necessity of undertaking a dangerous voyage by land or sea. Thus it seems right to begin the journey on the Thames, and Caversham Lock, conveniently close to Reading Station, makes a good starting point.

The first locks on the River Thames were simple flash locks, but these were difficult to use and wasted water, so, bit by bit, they were replaced by pound locks. Caversham Lock, which is mentioned in documents as early as the 15th century, was converted to a pound lock in 1778. Rebuilt in 1875, it is a good example of a typical Thames lock, with a lock-keeper to work the large, hydraulically operated gates. Today, its setting has changed little, for despite Reading reinventing itself as a bustling modern business centre, with towering blocks of modern architecture such as the Blade and the Oracle, any attempt to develop the water meadows past which the Thames flows has so far been met with stern resistance.

Continuing east along the towpath for about a mile, the traveller finally reaches Kennet Mouth, where the River Kennet meets the Thames. The traveller is immediately confronted with a plethora of bridges. Attached to the railway bridge of 1841 is the Horseshoe Bridge – a timber and girder construction which dates from 1891 and replaced a ferry. It was built for horses to reach the towpath on the other side – now it is more likely to be used by cyclists and pedestrians. Once across it, and approaching the railway bridge, one sees the first glimpse of Kennetside, now obscured by a footbridge which also carries a pipe. This was added when the gasworks spread to both sides of the river.

The houses and school on Kennetside looked out over an industrial scene, where many of the inhabitants must have

Above: Looking upstream towards Caversham Lock a century ago. The lock entrance is to the left, with the weir on the right.

Left: County Lock, Reading, October 1974.

Kennetside in the early 1900s. Many of the houses would have been homes for workers at Huntley & Palmers.

worked. Today, much of that industry has gone, and with it many of the houses, although some have been replaced by new homes. This section is still officially part of the River Thames, and Blake's Lock is under the jurisdiction of the Environment Agency, who administer all the non-tidal Thames Locks. Although it is not, therefore, really part of the canal, this cut was made when the Kennet was made navigable. The old river wound its way around the other side of the lock island.

One of Reading's lost industries is biscuit-making. Thanks to Huntley & Palmers, Reading became known as Biscuit Town, and the works which began in a small shop in 1826 eventually occupied much of the land on the other side of the river, upstream of Blake's Lock. Waterborne transport was ideal for moving their products around, thus cutting down on breakages, and the canal was a gateway to the West of England market for them. At dinnertime, the streets around the factory filled with workers hurrying home for their break. Today, just one building is left, beside the road bridge which crosses the canal, to remind us of this mammoth enterprise.

The cut rejoins the old river which can be seen disappearing northwards on the far side of the stream. A diversion this way, using the footbridge, would take you to the remains of Reading Abbey, whose monks were the first people to use the River Kennet as a handy marina for

Huntley and Palmer's Biscuit Factory, Reading.

Clockwise from opposite page top left:
Kennet Mouth.

Looking upstream from Kennet Mouth about 1900.

The same view today.

The remains of the once magnificent Reading Abbey.

The Abbey Gateway, where Jane Austen went to school.

Behind the Norman arches of the Abbey loom the towers of Reading Gaol.

High Bridge, rebuilt in 1787 to allow larger boats to use the Kennet Navigation.

In 1929, the steam barge *Swan* smashes through ice as she passes Crane Wharf.

(Inset) Crane Wharf today. These old houses can just be seen behind Swan's funnel, in the previous photograph.

Huntley & Palmers' factory around 1910.

Blake's Lock, improved from a simple flashlock into a pound lock in 1802.

boats travelling up and down the Thames, thus making Reading an inland port. There is little to see today, but anyone of a literary persuasion may wish to make a pilgrimage to a place which has associations with several authors, one being Hilaire Belloc. In his book *The Historic Thames*, he lamented the destruction of the Abbey during the dissolution of the monasteries, saying that its loss was irreplaceable.

In the Middle Ages the monks produced a manuscript which contains one of the earliest songs known in English – 'Sumer is icumen in'. The restored Inner Gateway was once a school which a very young Jane Austen attended for a while. She was probably too young to gain much from it, but where her elder sister Cassandra went, Jane determinedly followed. Beyond the Abbey can be seen the grim towers of Reading Gaol where Oscar Wilde was incarcerated. The path, Chestnut Walk, beside the old River Kennet, has been dedicated to him as a memorial.

The land on the west side of the old River Kennet, as it left the cut, is called Crane Wharf. Today, this area has gone upmarket, with a Belgian bar and apartment complexes, but as late as the mid-twentieth century this was still very much a working area. Just a couple of the old houses survive. Now painted in light colours and somewhat gentrified, they are dwarfed by the towering blocks which are the latest manifestation of Reading's ability to reinvent itself to suit

Right: An aerial view of Simonds' Brewery around 1875 gives no clue as to how winding this section of the navigation is. Bridge Street runs along the bottom of the picture, the brewer's house is in the centre, and the River Kennet is to the right.

Far right: Looking south from Seven Bridges Wharf, just west of Bridge Street Bridge, in 1820. The church is that of St Giles.

the times. Yet their moorings, now occupied by private narrowboats, remind us that this was once a busy wharf.

Despite the Kennet Navigation opening in the 1720s, High Bridge was as far upstream as large boats could come, for, despite its name, it was too low to allow them to pass beneath it. In 1787 it was replaced by the present bridge, whose headroom is still not generous.

Beyond High Bridge, the river was owned by the Kennet & Avon Canal Company (K&ACC). The bridge marks the entrance to the dreaded Brewery Gut – notorious among the boating community for being narrow, winding and fast-flowing. Over the years, Simonds' Brewery encroached on the towpath, making navigation difficult. Even today, with the area opened up, this section is controlled by traffic lights. The brewery buildings were designed by Sir John Soane, but only Seven Bridges House – William Simonds' own home – survives to give us an idea of how it must have looked when first built in the late 1780s.

After World War II, it was Bridge Street Bridge that became a problem to users of the canal. In 1947, John Gould, famous among Kennet & Avon enthusiasts for his role in saving the canal from closure, brought two boats along the canal from Saltford, en route for Wargrave. At Bridge Street

Bridge, it was discovered that girders had been installed beneath the bridge to strengthen it, reducing the headroom to 4 feet 6 inches (1.4m). Gould got the boats through when Reading Corporation agreed to lower the water level, using Blake's Weir. Other boats had been turned back.

It was a very different story in the canal's heyday. In 1820, someone standing on Seven Bridges Wharf, just west of the bridge, would have witnessed a busy scene, with boats moored at the wharf, and goods being loaded and unloaded on to carts and barrows on the wharf across the river.

Cross the bridge to the other side of the river, and walk along Seven Bridges Wharf – now looking very unwharflike. Such wharfs extended right up through Reading on the River Kennet. Beyond Seven Bridges Wharf was Bear Wharf, where there was once a basin as well as the original County Lock. The basin was filled in and the lock moved to its present position in the mid 1870s. Matters were made worse in the 1880s when the GWR, by then owners of the canal, sold part of the towpath here to the brewery, which closed it. Walkers had to rejoin the path through an alley off Fobney Street. In the first decade of the twentieth century, a single-track railway came down from the main line to a goods yard nearby, with sidings at Bear Wharf,

Some of the brewery buildings at Bear Wharf in 1955. The top gate of County Lock is in the foreground, and the maltings are in the distance.

These three photographs of County Lock were taken from roughly the same spot in 1898, 1982, and 2009. Apart from the fact that the brewery was taken over by Courage, there is little difference between the first two. By 1982, however, the brewery had already moved to a greenfield site outside Reading, and by the time the third photograph was taken almost all the brewery buildings had been demolished. Those that remain have been converted and the Oracle shopping centre fills the main site.

serving Simonds' Brewery and the Jamworks. The sidings went in 1969, and the whole line closed in 1983.

Sadly, the curtain came down on Reading as a brewing town in 2010, when Scottish & Newcastle, its owners, closed the brewery down. However, as real ale drinkers know, while the large breweries struggle, micro-breweries are flourishing, and there are some in Reading and the nearby area. So perhaps this trade – unlike biscuit-making – may yet return.

'One does not linger in the neighbourhood of Reading.' So wrote Jerome K Jerome in *Three Men in a Boat*. However, Reading is reluctant to let you escape its clutches and reach open countryside. The place has grown, and new industries and new roads have closed in on the canal. At Fobney, the waterworks have made the lock awkward for boaters, but there is a sense that the town has been shaken off, although a developer is keen to build houses on the watermeadows.

After passing Southcote Lock, where the Milkmaid's Bridge crosses over to the former pumping station, moored narrowboats start to appear, indicating that Burghfield Island – a rather exclusive set of moorings – is not far away.

The towpath passes beneath Burghfield Bridge. The first bridge here was a simple wooden affair, built in the thirteenth century – the main arch you see today dates from around 1812, and was probably designed by John Rennie, engineer to the K&ACC, although the brick arches to the north may be part of a Tudor bridge.

The name of the nearby pub, The Cunning Man, refers to a local story about a wise man or wizard who lived at nearby Tadley in the mid-eighteenth century, and helped protect people from dark spirits and witches.

A little further on comes Burghfield Lock. The original turf-sided lock now forms the entrance to the

Burghfield Bridge around 1910. The scene has changed little in the hundred years since this photograph was taken.

In 1982 (top left) Garston Lock was looking rather overgrown, but in 1994 (top right) four years after the Queen had once again declared the K&A fully open, it was looking rather smart. The pill boxes had been spruced up, there was new brickwork, the grass was neatly cut and the shrubs cut back. Fifteen years on, in 2009 (below), the graffiti artists had spray-painted the pill boxes, one of which was nearly submerged under Old Man's Beard; nature was once again taking a determined hold on Garston Lock, and it looked a little dejected.

main lock, which was built upstream of the old one in 1968.

Shortly after this, the modern age once again intrudes on the scene as the M4 crosses on a high flyover, but after this the surroundings seem surprisingly rural, even though the outskirts of Reading are not far away. The next lock, Garston, is the only surviving turf-sided lock in use on the entire canal. After Newbury barges ceased to be used, the Great Western Railway altered and strengthened it by using old pieces of railway line and large slabs of Welsh slate. Turf-sided locks are not easy to use, which is why, in the restoration, most were rebuilt as conventional locks, but Garston never closed so it remains today.

It is guarded by two pill-boxes. These were built in World War II, when the K&A was declared to be the Blue Defence Line. Pillboxes, tank traps and other MoD buildings were erected along its length, some of which survive, as they do here – they are, in fact, listed. However, if Hitler's armies had made it across the English Channel, it is hard to see how a canal was going to stop them in their tracks, so it is just as well it was never tested.

Despite its peaceful setting, the next lock has generated a certain amount of controversy. Niall Allsop, in his guide to the canal, calls it the lock with two names – Shenfield or Sheffield. Many boaters still refer to it as Shenfield, although Wikipedia tells us sternly that this is incorrect. It is true that not far away is Sheffield Bottom – but the nearby mill is called Shenfield Mill. Refusing to get embroiled in this, let us look instead at the strange shape of the lock sides.

Originally this was a turf-sided lock, but about 1760 it was enlarged to take the larger Newbury barges. Scalloped brickwork was introduced for the sides, though it only came partially up the lock wall – the upper section remained turf-sided. In 1980, the brickwork was continued up to the top of the lock wall. No one seems quite sure why this scalloping was done. Was it to strengthen the walls or was it, as some have suggested, to cut down turbulence as the lock filled?

At one time, the words Theale Swing Bridge were enough to strike terror into a boater's heart, and many cruises from Reading ended at Sheffield, as boats turned rather than face the effort of shifting the bridge. To raise it off its chocks involved turning a large wheel an interminable number of times, while angry lorry drivers revved their engines, or even drove over it while it was being lifted, causing it to bounce alarmingly.

Ran Meinertzhagen, who operated a passenger boat on this stretch in the late 1950s, recalls that, 'it took hours to jack up and was heavy to push open. One lunchtime, we unfortunately managed to have the bridge stuck open, and a lot of the people who worked in the pen factory on the other side of the river couldn't get back for the afternoon shift.'

Today there is a modern electrically operated bridge, which copes much better with the traffic, although many drivers still show signs of irritation at being held up for a few minutes while a narrowboat or two glides gracefully by.

Shenfield – or Sheffield – Lock.

This was the peaceful scene at Theale a hundred years ago.

Above: Just north of Theale swing bridge was the old canal inn, the Bridge House, then a Simonds' pub but now a private house.

Top right: These cottages at Theale are now desirable residences.

Right: As recently as 1937, this was the face of agriculture in this part of Berkshire.

Although, even today, the scene is still quite rural, appearances can be deceptive. Reading has spread its tentacles, and, despite Theale determinedly fighting to keep its village atmosphere, it is fast becoming a dormitory town for its large neighbour. Canalside cottages have been gentrified and extended. Yet before World War II, this was very much an agricultural area, with farming methods which had changed little for centuries.

The next lock, Sulhamstead, is, to the uninitiated, rather ugly, but it marks the return of the K&A from dereliction to a viable canal. In 1965, the K&A Trust paid for Sulhamstead to be made usable once more. To help achieve this aim, volunteers were recruited from the army and from Oxford and Winchester prisons. Although later restorations gave locks a more traditional appearance, this very basic repair has proved extremely durable.

At the next swing bridge and lock, Tyle Mill, not a great deal has changed in the last century except for the bridge itself – now modernised, with the lock rebuilt in 1976.

Tyle Mill Lock.

Sulhamstead Lock.

Tyle Mill Bridge.

Collectors of unusual pub names would once have wanted to detour to the north to see the Three Kings – Jack's Booth, on the A4. The most likely reason for this curious name was that one landlord, Jack Jones, organised fist-fights there. Regrettably, those recently refurbishing the pub saw fit to do away with this unique name, renaming it The Spring – and thus another little piece of local history dies.

Architectural enthusiasts, however, will want to detour south, to see if they can catch a glimpse of Folly Farm, originally a seventeenth-century house which was first altered and added to by Edwin Lutyens in 1906. Over the years, subsequent owners recalled Lutyens to make further additions, and in 1916 the Lutyens family lived here for a short time. Gertrude Jekyll came to visit, and the gardens she helped Lutyens to create are said to be one of their finest collaborations. However, Folly Farm is mainly hidden away behind hedges and walls, and it is only possible to catch glimpses of this extraordinary house. Little touches like the characteristically curved steps and occasional circular openings in the wall give the game away that this is a Lutyens and Jekyll collaboration, however.

Folly Farm, showing both the old house and the Lutyens extension.

The swing bridge at Aldermaston around 1905, with the brewery beyond.

The towpath continues to wander along the river valley, changing sides at Ufton, where it passes the degated Ufton Lock. This was added in 1830 to improve the head of water at Towney Lock upstream. With its rise and fall of only 1 ft 9 inches (54 cms), it was considered expendable during restoration, especially after Towney was rebuilt as a conventional lock.

Padworth was successfully converted from a turf-sided lock in 1984. It is now most

notable for an old canal milestone, discovered during dredging in the cut between here and Aldermaston Wharf. It has now been erected here, although the distances on it suggest that this was not its original site.

The next stop is Aldermaston Wharf. The village of Aldermaston is over a mile away, but the station is just north of the canal.

Approaching the bridge, there are, on the far side of the cut, some old malthouses, and, on the near side, firstly the wharfinger's house and then the K&A Trust shop and tearoom in an old canal worker's cottage. It is a very peaceful spot – but it was not always so.

Beyond the bridge was the old Strange's Brewery, demolished in the 1950s. The bridge itself was replaced by a bascule bridge in 1981, despite this section not being navigable. The swing bridge had been fixed for some time, but was becoming unsafe. Three years were to pass, however, before the lock was restored, and the section was not opened until 1987, when Padworth Swing Bridge was replaced.

In 1982, the lock, its turf sides still with their protective old GWR railway lines, was choked with vegetation, and an ugly pipe ran from the works behind the lock across to the other side. Only the brickwork at gate level suggested that this, like Sheffield (or Shenfield) had scalloped walls. The restoration proved that this was the case. After removing the timbers which had once provided the structure for the turf sides – and which, according to one workman, were still

Far left, top: Aldermaston Lock in 1982, unrestored and unusable.

Far left, below: Restoration under way in August 1984.

Left: The restored lock in 1994.

almost intact – the scalloped walls were continued to the top of the lock, with a line of blue bricks marking the change between old and new, the pipe was removed, and gates refitted. It looks superb.

Just downstream of the lock, a short arm heads off towards the railway line. At this point, the GWR came very close to the canal. Stuck with a canal it did not really want, the GWR made the best of it by installing a transhipment point here. Today the arm is partly filled in, and what remains is a quiet backwater, although it is a convenient place to moor up while taking on water and pumping out.

Dealing with the many bridges was one of the problems facing those restoring the canal. Froude's Swing Bridge had long been fixed, and was replaced with a brick bridge in 1990.

A little further upstream, after walking through some delightful countryside, the towpath changes sides on Wickham Knights Bridge. Once a swing bridge, it was replaced with a wheelchair-and-cycle-friendly bridge with

Froude's Bridge, rebuilt in 1990.

The new Wickham Knights Bridge.

long ramps. It is less picturesque, perhaps, but opens the towpath to many more users.

Shortly after this, Woolhampton Swing Bridge makes its appearance. Just across the bridge, on the way to the village, was the Rose and Crown – long closed. This bridge has also been replaced with an electrically-operated bridge which, though more utilitarian, is stronger and better able to cope with today's traffic.

Although the Rose and Crown has gone, the Rowbarge, on the other side of the bridge, remains. Blatch's Brewery, which supplied the Rose and Crown, was based at Theale, but was absorbed into Ind Coope in 1965.

Shortly above the bridge, the navigation leaves the river to the south and enters another cut. An attractive horse bridge once crossed here, and the scene downstream has proved attractive to artists and photographers over the years.

The old Woolhampton Swing Bridge and the Rose and Crown.

Woolhampton today, with the new bridge in use.

The Rose and Crown, with Woolhampton Bridge and the Rowbarge in the distance.

Woolhampton was a popular spot for photographers. A Southampton postcard publisher produced this picture looking eastwards, back towards the swing bridge, with a horse bridge in the foreground.

The lock was still operative as late as 1928, as CH Smith, in his account of a journey up the K&A, makes clear. However, judging by the fact that holiday crowds watched them all the way through, it seems a boat was a rare sight.

By 1982, Woolhampton Lock was a sorry sight – its chamber completely choked with weeds, and a wartime pillbox blocking the operation of the gates. Restoration began in the mid 1980s by rebuilding a traditional pound lock more or less inside the old lock. During these works, more evidence of the original structure of the lock was found. After careful deliberation, it was decided that the pillbox would have to go.

Where possible, swing bridges were retained in their original form. In 1982, Oxleaze swing bridge looked as it had done for centuries. A careful copy of the old bridge has left us with an unaltered scene, but a fully working bridge.

Woolhampton Lock when it was still a working turf-sided lock, about 1920. Perhaps the artist in this picture was painting the scene in the previous photograph.

Woolhampton Lock, derelict and degated, with a WWII pillbox, in 1982.

Woolhampton Lock in the mid 1980s, with restoration work well advanced.

In 1982, Oxleaze Swing Bridge looked as it had done for two centuries, with only the diamond-shaped GWR warning sign to show that it no longer belonged to the K&ACC.

Oxleaze Swing Bridge in 2009. Restoration was necessary, but the bridge style has been copied. Only the new bridge moorings show that there have been changes.

Midgham Lock before restoration, November 1987.

Heale's Lock being completely excavated and rebuilt.

Various methods were tried out when restoring the locks. At Heale's, the old turf-sided lock was completely dug out, leaving a large hole in the ground within which the new lock was rebuilt in 1989.

A mile and a half on from Heale's Lock, the scene becomes decidedly industrial, especially after the rather daunting Midgham Lock Bridge. This was once the site of a large paper mill.

Paper-making in Colthrop began as early as 1740, when a fulling mill was converted to paper-making. With a plentiful supply of water, and the Kennet Navigation for transport, it was clearly an ideal situation. Over the years, the mill grew,

The paper mills at Colthrop (above), where the publisher has misspelt the name, and the canal at Thatcham (below) on postcards from around 1906.

although its fortunes sometimes fluctuated. By the early twentieth century, the works covered a large area, and during World War I the company began to make cardboard. About this time it must have looked rather curious to have a large factory, with its tall chimneys, in an otherwise rural landscape. Paper-making ceased in 1971, and the space is now given over to industrial units.

Another swing bridge that has been replaced with a fixed up-and-over bridge is at Thatcham, where the banks have also been tidied up considerably. The canalside peace and quiet hides the fact that Thatcham is now an extension of Newbury, with housing estates and ribbon development along the A4.

We are now well embarked on the Long Cut, and the scenery is attractive and peaceful. It is a pity, therefore, that one is confronted with one of the disasters of the restoration, Monkey Marsh Lock.

The lock itself is pleasantly situated among the meandering tributaries of the Kennet, through which the Long Cut takes a direct course. It was yet another turf-sided lock, no different in its way from the others we have met. Certainly Garston was the best surviving example. Without telling anyone, someone quietly got Monkey Marsh Lock listed. When it came to restoration, there was an impasse between English Heritage, who insisted that it be retained, and British Waterways who said, rightly, that turf-sided locks were dangerous, particularly with leisure boaters using the canal, and could not be permitted. Garston had only survived because it did not need repair.

To cut a long story short, an unhappy compromise was reached, the only beneficial outcome of which seems to have been the thorough archaeological investigation which revealed much new information about the development of these locks. Sadly, what is there now is neither a turf-sided lock nor like anything else you will see on any canal anywhere. At the time, comments in *The Butty*, the magazine of the K&A Trust, were fairly acid. It has now become the trust's policy to put a brave face on it, and be polite, even complimentary, but in truth the lock is a beast – unpleasant to use and to look upon. When the water level is high, and the edges overgrown, as they are now, it is not too bad, but, when the lock empties, onlookers are left gazing at grubby, green-stained concrete. It is a salutary lesson in what can

The approach to the turf-sided Monkey Marsh Lock as it appeared in the early twentieth century.

Today, this is the unhappy compromise between British Waterways and English Heritage – a lock that looks like nothing else on the entire canal. Its edges have softened with vegetation since this photograph was taken in 1994, but it remains an unsatisfactory solution.

Widmead Lock in 1982 – sinking into oblivion.

happen when two groups involved in a single project – in this case British Waterways and English Heritage – suddenly find they have different agendas. Meanwhile, the third party – the K&A Trust – was left, a helpless and frustrated bystander, squeezed between two government agencies, neither of which wanted to give way or make a sensible compromise.

Further up the cut, Widmead Lock was restored more conventionally, and now looks very different from the dereliction of 1982.

After Widmead, the railway, which has been on the right, changes sides. Beyond the railway bridge lies Bull's Lock – our first indication that we are nearing Newbury. It was restored by volunteer labour in 1976 under BWB supervision. Shortly after this, the trades union imposed an embargo on working with volunteers, on the grounds that

At Bull's Lock, near Newbury, the house has gone, but the gongoozlers – canal speak for idle bystanders – remain. The River Lambourne joins the Kennet here, on the right.

they were taking work from members, and so Bull's Lock remains the only one repaired under this scheme.

The towpath changes sides on the unlovely Ham Bridge, which replaced a swing bridge. Given the amount of traffic you have to negotiate to cross the bridge, you can see why it was felt necessary to replace it. There are ramps here for cyclists and wheelchairs. The path is shaded by trees, and it is hard to believe that local industry is just the other side of the fence, although it has long been an industrial site. On the far side of Ham Lock is an industrial estate, formerly the site of Ham Mills.

At last one comes to Greenham Lock. Although it was restored using steel piling in 1972, its setting is one of the most attractive on the whole canal – which is extraordinary, considering its urban surroundings.

Just upstream of the lock, on the left bank, is the site of Greenham Mill, now given over to housing which looks vaguely like mill buildings. There had been mills here for centuries, and, by the eighteenth century, they were mainly

Greenham Lock in 1976 after restoration, with the old bridge on the right.

Greenham Lock in 2009. The rebuilt bridge spans the entrance to a marina.

The crane and the K&A Trust building at Newbury Wharf.

The first of these two postcard views of the Cloth Hall at Newbury shows it in the early twentieth century, when it was still being used for storage. The second view shows it in the 1950s, when the wharf had become a bus station and the ground floor had been converted to shops.

involved in the wool trade. By the early nineteenth century, however, the wool trade in the south and west was in decline, faced with competition from northern mills. John Coxeter, of Greenham, had installed up-to-date machinery in his mill, and casually told a local landowner, Sir John Throckmorton, that he believed he could make a coat in the hours of daylight, from the wool being shorn from a sheep in the morning to a tailor completing the coat by the evening. Sir John, convinced that Coxeter knew what he was talking about, laid a wager of 1,000 guineas among his friends, backing the mill-owner. There is no doubt it was intended to boost the Newbury cloth trade. Sir John won his wager with three hours to spare, and the event was celebrated at a dinner later in the evening. Sir John wore the coat and the main course was mutton – from the sheep which had provided the wool. Despite this success, the wool trade still declined.

Eventually, the towpath goes under a very low road bridge to reach the site of the old canal basin, completely filled in to make a bus station, which, when the buses left, became a car park. One of the helpful information boards found along the canal, gives us an idea of how the basin once looked. The small stone building, the last remnant of the wharf complex and now stranded rather forlornly among the cars and bollards, is owned by the K&A Trust. The old crane also survives.

One relic of Newbury's cloth trade survives on the far side of the car park. It was once the cloth hall. Still used for storage a hundred years ago, it was later converted to shops and now houses Newbury's museum.

At this point, we have reached the limit of the Kennet Navigation. The next chapter takes us along the canal constructed in the closing years of the eighteenth century and the first decade of the nineteenth century.

4 Newbury to Crofton: Uphill All the Way

Newbury is an interesting and historic town, where the traveller may wish to wander for a time. Even if you do not want to stray far from the canal, it is worth visiting the museum in the old cloth hall, and also the small collection of canal-related items in the Kennet & Avon Canal Trust building on the wharf, where there are also refreshments. Newbury also has many pubs, cafés and restaurants, for those who want something more than tea, sandwiches and cake.

The canal has been climbing very gently ever since Reading, and that gentle climb continues until reaching the Crofton flight, when, with nine locks to pass, the pace quickens a little until we reach Crofton Top Lock and the Kennet & Avon's summit level. In addition, although now on the canal proper, the River Kennet still winds its way in and out of the canal until it heads north at Hungerford, while the K&A heads south.

Heading west from Newbury Wharf, the towpath comes to an abrupt end where the Town Bridge crosses the canal. The pedestrian climbs a ramp to cross the road and descend on the other side, but what happens if you are in a boat, making your way upstream? If you have an engine, there is no problem, but when horses provided the motive power, there was.

The solution was this: the boat had to moor up while the captain uncoupled the horse, and led him up and across the street, which even then was busy with traffic. They continued down a ramp and over a bridge – once an attractive wooden affair, though later replaced with something more durable – to reach the lock At the lock the captain attached the end of the rope to a float which was kept there. He tossed this into the water, where it floated under the bridge, to be caught by the crew and reconnected to the boat. The horse had then

to give a mighty pull to bring the boat under the bridge and into the lock. This lengthy procedure was clearly too much for some captains, who hauled across the street, so that a

Top: Looking over the bridge down Bridge Street and into Northbrook Street. Today, there are restrictions on vehicular access, so there is now less traffic than can be seen here.

Above: Looking up towards Newbury Lock, when the lock-keeper's cottage was still in use. A barge waits in the lock, while the horse stands at the side.

Opposite: Town Bridge, Newbury, c1910.

Picturesque Berkshire
THE TOWN BRIDGE, NEWBURY.

THE BRIDGE AND RIVER KENNET, NEWBURY.

Left: An artistic view from around 1900 looking east towards Town Bridge.

Bottom left: A postcard published some twenty years later, with no sign of working boats, only pleasure craft.

Below left: The history of the K&A, painted by LTC Rolt, on the lock-keepers cottage at Newbury.

Below, top right: The float to which the tow-rope had to be attached. In 1982, it was still at the lock – now it is kept for safety in the K&A collection of Newbury memorabilia at the Stone House.

Below, bottom right: The sign warning captains about penalties if they towed across the bridge, still in its original position before the fire which destroyed the cottage in 1989.

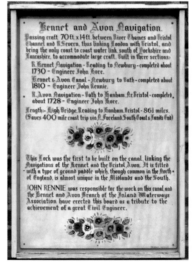

sign had to be put up, warning them of the consequences if they continued.

The sign, along with other memorabilia, including a history of the canal painted by LTC Rolt, used to be displayed on the lock-keeper's cottage which stood here. In 1982, it stood empty, its doors and windows blocked up, and John Gould was fearful for its future. His fears were justified. On 18 October 1989 it was mysteriously destroyed by fire, exactly

as he had predicted. The various artefacts once displayed here can now be seen at the K&A Trust building on the wharf.

Newbury Lock is unusual for the K&A in that the paddles on the top gates are worked by levers rather than by winding gear. This system is common on northern canals, but not in the south.

Shortly after the lock comes West Mills Wharf, which is reached by crossing the West Mills Swing Bridge. Having crossed, the path then goes past some very old weavers' cottages, which were used in the late eighteenth century to house the navvies who were constructing the canal. From here can be seen the tower of St Nicholas's Church, dating from 1532. The church was begun by John Smalwoode, who later adopted the surname Winchcombe, but is known as Jack of Newbury. He rose to become one of the wealthiest clothiers in the country. After he died, his son, also John, completed the church.

When railway mania seized the country, it seemed as though the day of the canal had passed. Yet, as we shall see,

Above: The unusual lever-operated paddles in use at Newbury Lock. The man in a duffel coat, with his head turned away from the camera, is John Gould.

Top right: In this final glimpse of Newbury Lock, there are two Newbury barges moored above the lock. The cottage is to the left of the picture and the sign warning captains is just visible.

Centre right: West Mills Wharf, with a laden barge moored up. On the right is a salt, slate and coal warehouse. It is not clear if the little group of people are the ship's captain's family or if they are waiting to cadge a lift. St Nicholas's Church can be seen in the distance.

Bottom right: Looking in the other direction we can see the old weavers' cottages, used in the late eighteenth century to house navvies.

Another view of West Mills Wharf from further west, showing the swing bridge. A little girl appears to be an early pioneer for cycling the towpath.

Before heading west, we take a final glimpse back at Newbury.

The bridge abutment at West Mills; the bridge carrying the Newbury Bypass; and the (amended) Concrete Society Award.

the canal has outlasted several railways that passed near it. A brick abutment about half a mile on from West Mills is all that survives of a railway bridge where the Lambourn Valley Railway (operational from 1898 to 1973) crossed the canal after leaving the main line. It has been replaced by a new bridge, which you encounter just after Guyer's Lock, where the towpath changes sides. This carries not a railway but the controversial Newbury Bypass. Although the Concrete Society granted it an award, someone has hijacked the plaque to remind us that roads come at an environmental cost – in this case, 10,000 trees.

After the main line has crossed the canal once more, the way lies through the delightful wooded and watery area known as Benham Broad. It is not a natural landscape. Like Wilcot Wide Water, which we will come to later, it is part of a scene originally landscaped by Lancelot 'Capability' Brown

This engraving of Benham Park appears to have been drawn by someone sitting on the canal bank. The Kennet and the lake are both visible. The canal was intended to enhance the Arcadian scene created by Lancelot 'Capability' Brown. Today, however, the view is blocked by the railway embankment.

for the owner of Benham Park, William, Lord Craven. Brown's son-in-law, Henry Holland, was the architect of the house. When the canal was built, Craven promoted it, and was in a good position to insist it should look aesthetically pleasing in the landscape. After he died, his widow married the Margrave of Anspach, who bought the property from Craven's heir.

A little way further on, at Hamstead Lock, is a view of a delightful mill. It was built in 1810, after 'a conflagration of a most destructive character' destroyed the previous mill. This was part of the Craven estate, and given its elegant appearance, with an octagonal main building, it appears that the then Lord Craven was also keen on picturesque landscapes. The Kennet Horse Boat Company's barge *Kennet Valley* can sometimes be seen along this stretch, between Newbury and Kintbury.

Next comes the aptly named Copse Lock, set among overhanging trees. About two miles after Copse Lock, and after passing Dreweatt's Lock and the rather fine Shepherd's Bridge, the bridge at Kintbury comes into view. Across the canal can be seen the Dundas Arms. Built in the eighteenth century as a house, it later became an inn, taking its name from Charles Dundas, first chairman of the Kennet & Avon Canal Company. He was from Scotland but came into possession of the estates here through his wife. He died in 1832 after contracting cholera. His monument is in the church. The inn was equipped with extensive stables, which became garages when motor transport took over. They have since been converted to hotel rooms.

After climbing up to the bridge and crossing the road, the traveller reaches Kintbury Lock. Despite its rural situation, this was a busy wharf, where goods such as flour, malt, hops and whiting – a fine chalk used in the

manufacture of paint – were loaded and off-loaded. The site of the whiting works was just south of Shepherd's Bridge.

The railway is very close to the canal here, so goods could be transhipped. By the 1880s, however, coal, once the most important commodity carried by the canal, was

The mill at Hamstead – all part of Lord Craven's picturesque landscape.

Bonnie the horse takes a welcome break as *Kennet Valley* enters Hamstead Lock. The coloured bobbins along the traces are not decorative, but prevent the leather from rubbing. It is also traditional for the horse to wear blinkers.

Copse Lock is still as wooded and faintly mysterious as it was when Ashton C Allen brought his steam launch *Eva* along the canal about 1890.

Above: *Kennet Valley* at Dreweatt's Lock in May 1972.

Below:The bridge at Kintbury, with the lock just beyond it. The bridge has been rebuilt with railings insead of brick parapets.

The Dundas Arms, named after Charles Dundas, around 1905.

The Dundas Arms after the stables had been converted to garages. A forlorn-looking horse peers out, doubtless wondering where his comfortable stable has gone.

Kintbury Church, with the Dundas memorial to the left of the chancel arch.

being moved around the country by rail. Here at Kintbury there was a substantial goods yard – it is now the station car park.

Many of the changes along the canal over the years have been caused by creeping urbanisation. Here, though, the change has been caused by trees growing up on both sides of the canal between the lock and Vicarage Bridge, obscuring the views which could once be had along this stretch.

At some time when the GWR owned the canal, Vicarage Bridge appears to have been damaged. The GWR repaired it by using some old railway line. It might have been a bit of a bodged job, but it has lasted till today. Beyond it is the old vicarage, now the home of successful writers, Robert Harris and his wife, Gill Hornby.

The towpath continues through woods for about a mile and a half, diving under bridges, including another main-line railway bridge, and past two more locks – Brunsden's and Wire. The towpath changes sides again over the bridge at Dun Mill, where the border of trees and bushes moves back from the canal edge to give a view along the southern side. At this point, the railway, canal and the rivers Dun and Kennet are very close.

Just over another half mile brings you to Hungerford and what was once a swing bridge – quite a hefty one, if

The canal at Kintbury around 1910. Tall trees now obscure the view and the mill has been converted to apartments.

Looking east from Vicarage Bridge at around the same time. This view is now completely obscured by trees on both sides.

Damage to Vicarage Bridge was repaired by the GWR using old railway lines – they are still there today.

Many pictures of the Vicarage were taken in the early twentieth century. The vicar at the time must have had a family who were enthusiastic rowers, because all of them feature young people messing about in boats.

Kintbury Lock in the 1890s, with a crowd of onlookers admiring *Eva*. As the number of working boats declined, so gentlemen like Ashton C Allen and Charles Penruddocke took to making leisure cruises on the canal. Little could they have known that they were setting the pattern for the future. The wagons in the background belong to the Radstock Coal Company, which by then had switched from canal to rail. The haystack is standing in what is now part of the car park.

Denford Mill, Hungerford.

At Dun Mill, the railway, canal and the Rivers Dun and Kennet are very close. On this Edwardian postcard showing men working on the railway, both Dun Mill – which appears to be on the canal but is actually on the Dun – and beyond it Denford Mill on the Kennet can be seen, as well as the canal and river bridges.

The canal flowing past Dun Mill – the river which powered the mill is out of sight to the right. The mill is still there, but a large weeping willow now hides it from view.

VIEW FROM THE COMMON HUNGERFORD

the pictures of it are to be believed. In 1928, CH Smith found it almost unmovable. It was only thanks to help from onlookers that he finally managed to shift it. It collapsed in the 1950s when Thames Conservancy staff tried to move a heavy excavator across it. It was replaced with a temporary footbridge which had to be removed every time a boat came along. The final replacement never arrived. The temporary bridge was raised up on bricks and still does service today.

The towpath goes under Town Bridge. When the canal was built, the roadway was raised up, and houses on either side of the bridge had to build bridges across to their front doors. Hungerford amply repays a visit. It has some interesting independent shops, a variety of pubs and restaurants, and many places to stay. Above all, it has some wonderful old buildings. What it does not have, as yet, is a museum, but it has a virtual museum on line at *www.hungerfordvirtualmuseum.co.uk*, which is a must for anyone who plans to spend time in Hungerford.

Among the list of historic buildings is the attractive row of cottages beside the canal. Now painted a dazzling white, with their beams blackened, it was not always so. The fad for painting timbered buildings white and the beams black is an Edwardian one. Originally such beams would probably have been covered in plaster or limewash.

On the other side of the canal from the cottages was the wharf, but the stretch of canal immediately in front of them was – and still is – used for a variety of activities. On a quiet day, it might have been a gentle bit of angling, but at times the Hungerford Swimming Sports were held here. In 1982, this stretch of water was still being used for leisure, such as canoeing classes.

Left: The swing bridge near Hungerford Station in the 1890s.

Bottom left: A postcard view of the bridge from around 1910.

Bottom right: After its collapse in the 1950s, the swing bridge was replaced by this temporary structure, which has now become permanent.

The wharf itself was a busy one, with loads of gravel, chalk and whiting heading west and timber heading east. With all the mills locally, and Hungerford being set in a fertile valley, grain and flour were also important exports. Meanwhile, coal and Bath stone were imported. Although trade on the canal dropped away in the late nineteenth century, Hungerford remained busy, as pictures of the wharf at various times show. They also show that much of the trade was timber. Even on a snowy day, with the canal frozen, work still continued. The stone building was a warehouse, now converted to two rather elegant houses, but the warehouse behind it has gone. Today, narrowboats moor up where once were working boats. However, even in those busy days, there were times when the boats carried local residents on outings, even though the trippers would have had to pick their way through the building materials of J Wooldridge & Sons, who ran the wharf for over a century.

Just beyond the wharf is Hungerford Lock. Once busy with boats coming and going to Hungerford, it fell into disrepair as the K&A was deliberately neglected, first of all by the GWR and then by the British Transport Commission, who actively discouraged people from using the canal. By

Top left: The Swimming Sports of August 1913 – a conventional race. There is a fireman on hand, presumably in case of accidents, and the bridge from the road into the cottage can be seen crammed with onlookers.

Centre left: The Swimming Sports of August 1913 – a 'fun run' type of race – though it would be frowned on today. This was the cigarette race, in which participants swam with a lighted cigarette in their mouths.

Bottom left: The canoe class of 1982 paddling about in the same stretch of water.

Top right: The cottages beside the canal at Hungerford before the Edwardian fad for painting the timbers of old buildings black and the infill white. It can be seen here how the road had to be raised when the bridge was built.

Bottom right: A more distant view, with the Station Road swing bridge, as it then was, visible through the bridge arch.

Above: Hungerford Wharf in the 1890s, with building materials stacked up.

Below left: A boat moored up by the stone warehouse, with felled trees, presumably delivered from Savernake Forest.

Below right: As late as 1895, the wharf was a busy place.

Right: Restoration under way in May 1972. The wooden warehouse has gone, but the stone waterhouse has been converted to housing.

Top left: Even in wintry weather, work continued, though it is not clear how far boats would get on the frozen canal.

Centre left: Hungerford Lock around 1910. The buildings to the right have been replaced by the houses at the end of Canal Walk.

Bottom left: By 1970, Hungerford Lock was in a parlous state, the lock gates unusable, the brickwork weed-infested.

Below: In the early twentieth century, an excited crowd of children set out on a celebratory trip in a working boat from Wooldridge & Sons' yard.

1970, the view eastwards from Hungerford Lock was one of complete dereliction. However, the restoration plan was already in hand, and the lock was fully restored by 1973.

As the towpath makes its way out of Hungerford, the parish church of St Lawrence is passed on the left, hidden among trees. It demonstrates dramatically the influence the canal had on building styles, for now the fashionable Bath stone could easily be brought eastwards. There are records of a church at Hungerford in 1147, but this Norman church was replaced by one in the Early English style sometime after 1208. By 1810, the crew of the sailing boat in the drawing on the opposite page might have noticed that it was roofless. By 1813 the cupola had fallen in and the tower was falling apart.

Above: A sailing boat passing the roofless church at Hungerford in 1810.

Below: Aston C Allen's photograph of the new church.

Work in progress near Hungerford church in the 1880s, as an Archimedes screw is used to drain water from a culvert under the canal. The trees that appear mere saplings here have now reached their full height.

In 1814, the decision was taken to rebuild it, using Bath stone. With the canal fully open it was a comparatively easy task, and the Canal Company must have been delighted to secure its largest contract so far. The parish council even employed a Bath architect, John Pinch the Elder, to design the church. However,

by 1880, alterations were made by John Wooldridge, the builder at Hungerford Wharf, and by the time Ashton C Allen came along in his steam launch *Eva*, the works were complete, allowing him to take the serene photograph on the left.

The route now lies across Freeman's Marsh, part of an area of outstanding natural beauty (AONB), and a site of special scientific interest (SSSI). It is also of interest to boaters because it has the famous – or perhaps notorious – Hungerford Marsh Lock. When the canal was built, a right of way for commoners existed precisely where it was necessary to build a lock. Rights of way were very highly regarded in those days – perhaps more so than they are now – and rerouting was not permitted. Therefore the lock chamber has a swing bridge right across it. Anyone negotiating this lock must swing the bridge first – or risk decapitation. Since this is common land where cattle graze, it may be necessary to persuade the cows who like to ensconce themselves on the slopes leading up to the bridge to relinquish their comfortable seat.

Shortly after this, there is another unusual lock, Cobbler's Lock. At first sight, it does not appear to be anything special, but if you follow a path leading down from the towpath to the meadows, you will soon discover that it is raised up on the first of the K&A aqueducts to be encountered on this journey, the Dun Aqueduct. Disappointingly, it is little more than a sluice – the ones near Bath get progressively more spectacular – but the scenery more than makes up for it, as the river ambles gently through the meadow below – another SSSI.

Just before the railway bridge, where once again the main line crosses the canal, there is a new wooden bridge. This replaced Barrackfield Swing Bridge and is probably now intended for the use of boats at the proposed Hungerford Marina – so far there is little sign of its completion. After Picketfield Lock, come the three Froxfield Locks – Lower,

Top left: Hungerford Marsh Lock.

Centre left: Cobbler's Lock in the early twentieth century.

Bottom left: The Dun aqueduct.

Below: The River Dun.

Middle and Oakhill Down. However, before passing these, those interested in history may wish to divert up the road towards Froxfield, to see the Duchess of Somerset's Hospital, founded in 1694 for the maintenance of 30 poor widows. The chapel was rebuilt in 1813, and is a classic little Georgian preaching box.

Returning to the canal, as the traveller heads westward, Berkshire is left behind, and from now on until the approach to Bath, we will be in Wiltshire. Look out for the ropemarks on the bridge at Oakhill Down Lock, which recall the days of horse-drawn boats.

The first village we come to is Little Bedwyn, where the railway is very close to the canal. The line arrived in 1862, built by a private company headed by Lord Ailesbury as a branch from Hungerford to Devizes. It now forms part of the main line from London to the south-west. Bedwyn station was built for the convenience of Lord Ailesbury, but it is at Great Bedwyn, not Little Bedwyn, which had a signal box but no station. When the line was upgraded in the late 1890s, it lost even that, and the road layout was drastically altered. The level crossing at Little Bedwyn was removed and the lane from Great Bedwyn carried over the line on a bridge to the west of the village. A pedestrian footbridge was put in at the same time, where the level crossing had been, and the swing bridge across the canal was removed. At the base of the footbridge, part of the original bridge over the stream can

Church Street, Little Bedwyn.

Little Bedwyn from Little Bedwyn Lock.

In order to take this picture of Little Bedwyn from a distance, Ashton C Allen, the owner of *Eva*, was probably standing on the lock gates of Potter's Lock. Today the view is obscured by road and rail bridges, as well as the trees which have grown up on either side of the canal.

still be seen. Yet, despite all this, the view along Church Street has remained unaltered – apart from the presence of parked cars.

The bridges now obscure the view back towards Little Bedwyn from Potter's Lock, as do the trees which have grown up alongside the canal.

Another mile on from Potter's Lock brings us to the outskirts of Great Bedwyn. On the left, where now there is a village hall in Frog Lane, there was once the Challenor-Ellis Hall. It was built in 1926 by the son of a Bedwyn doctor as a holiday retreat for children from Kilburn.

Directly opposite is the station, though it has lost its former attractive building, which has been replaced with something more utilitarian. Perhaps we should just be grateful that the station remains open. Locally, its survival is put down to the fact that Sir Felix Pole, born at Little Bedwyn and educated at Great Bedwyn School, where his father was the schoolmaster, later became general manager of the Great Western Railway.

Great Bedwyn has a remarkable twelfth-century church, and an equally remarkable Stonemasonry Museum, which

you pass on the way to the church. Until recently, this was still a working stone yard, and the buildings are covered in many examples of the stonemason's craft. The Lloyd family, to whom it belonged, owned the yard for centuries, and worked on building the Bruce Tunnel, further up the canal. The building now doubles as the post office. A self-guided walk around the village can be downloaded from *www.greatbedwyn.com*.

To continue the journey, anyone who has spent time in Great Bedwyn, if only to seek refreshment at either of the two

Great Bedwyn's village hall now stands on the site of this holiday retreat, built for poor children from Kilburn.

The twelfth-century church of St Mary's, Great Bedwyn.

The Stonemasonry Museum at Great Bedwyn, which now doubles as the post office.

A local train pulls out of Bedwyn station around 1910.

pubs, should return to the wharf. This is still recognisably a wharf, with an old wooden building still standing. The chief import here was cheap coal, for which the wharf was built. However, by interfering with the Bedwyn Brook, the canal killed the watermills. This is why Wilton Windmill – now open to the public – was erected in 1821.

From the towpath, there are glimpses of the church, with its solid tower topped by delicate tracery – not surprisingly, the next lock is called Church Lock. The canal then passes under a road bridge known as Mill Bridge, which is believed to be one of the first examples of skewing a bridge using brick and stone. Rennie perfected this technique, later used by IK Brunel with spectacular success, notably at Moulsford Bridge.

The next lock, Beech Grove, is also known as Crofton Bottom Lock. You have reached the start of your first flight of locks, at the end of which you will be at the highest point of the canal. Shortly after this lock comes the ruinous Bridge 99 – with the inappropriate name of New Bridge. Nicholas Hammond's map of 1975 even marks it as having gone – clearly he assumed that it would go in a very short

time. Yet, as an article in *The Butty* for March 1982 explains, it was built to align on two of the rides in the Marquis of Ailesbury's estate, so it has some historic interest.

At the next lock, Crofton Pumping Station comes into view. Although not quite at the highest point of the canal, if it is in steam – and you will be able to tell if smoke is issuing from its chimney – a visit will be the high point of your journey. To reach it, you have to cross the canal by the lock gates, and then dive under the railway via a tunnel – this is not a detour for anyone with vertigo or claustrophobia.

But first, look down to your left where you will see the artificial lake of Wilton Water. When the canal was first built, the problem of supplying water to the summit level seemed to have been solved when a number of springs were discovered in the area. Eventually, in 1836, the narrow valley was dammed, creating this reservoir.

The Pumping Station is run by a trust which has its own enthusiastic, knowledgeable and friendly guides, who will supply you with a wealth of information. But briefly, here is the story of the pumping station:

Mill Bridge.

Bridge 99 – the ruinous and inaptly named New Bridge.

Left: Crofton Pumping Station comes into view, the smoke from the chimney revealing that the boilers are in steam.

Below: The pumping station and the canal, with an express train rushing past. Though waterborne transport is slow, and rail is fast, both are more efficient than road for carrying goods – yet we use road.

Top left: Stoking the Lancashire boiler.

Above: The piston descends into the cylinder head. The brass cup introduces lubricating oil into the cylinders.

Left: The valve gear.

Top right: The Honeystreet Clock – rescued from the boatyard at Honeystreet, where parts of it were constructed from old farm machinery, it has now been faithfully restored.

Right: Each pump raises about one ton of water (just over 1000kg) per stroke, which then flows into the leat which feeds water to the summit level.

Crofton from the west.

To avoid building a four-mile-long tunnel from Crofton to Burbage, as proposed by Rennie, the canal company took advice from William Jessop who proposed raising the summit level to 458 feet (139m) above sea level and having a much shorter tunnel. However, this meant supplying the summit level with water from the springs in the valley below Crofton. This scheme was adopted, and the pumping station opened in 1807 with a secondhand but unused Boulton and Watt engine bought from the West India Dock Company. It had always been intended to have a second engine, and another Boulton and Watt engine was installed by 1810. In 1843, the boilers were replaced, and the first engine was replaced with a Sims Patent Combined Cylinder Engine supplied by Harveys of Hayle in Cornwall. Both engines continued in service until 1952. Today, water is pumped up from Wilton Water by electric pumps. However, the electric pumps have failed on occasion, with the old pumps called back into service until the problem was solved. If the building is open, there is an excellent café – the Engineman's Rest – and a shop.

Eventually, it is time to return to the canal, and leave the pumping station behind. Your last view of the pumping

station will be – like your first – of its tall chimney. This replaced an iron one in 1856, but by 1959 the top section was unsafe, and was removed. However, thanks to Sir John Smith, chairman of the Manifold Trust, funds were raised to restore it to its full height of 82 feet (25m). Sir John later recorded that it gave him pleasure every time he looked at it.

For industrial archaeology enthusiasts, there is more of interest as you continue up the flight. The Midland & South Western Junction Railway was formed in 1884 when the Swindon, Marlborough & Andover Railway and the Swindon & Cheltenham Extension Railway amalgamated. It crossed over the Berkshire & Hampshire Railway – the line which has accompanied us for much of our journey – and the junction – or what remains of it – lies just ahead.

The abutments below Lock 57 (above) and above Crofton Top Lock (below) – all that remains of the railway junctions between the M&SWJ and the main line.

The buttresses of the bridge carrying the branch to the main line towards Reading appear just below Lock 57. Two more locks bring us to Crofton Top Lock. Just beyond that are the remains of the bridge which carried the M&SWJR towards a junction with the main line going west, as well as northward towards Cheltenham.

After the final lock, we reach the summit level, the highest point of the canal. We have climbed about 350 feet (107m) and from now on, it is all along and downhill to Hanham, the end of the canal – a descent of about 400 feet (122m).

5 Crofton to Devizes: Mainly Plain Sailing

Beyond Crofton Top Lock, the towpath runs on, uninterrupted, for about a mile, while the banks on either side appear to rise up, so that eventually there is the sense of walking in a cutting. And then, just ahead, can be seen the dark portal of Bruce Tunnel, its mouth looking more ominous because of the heavy brickwork above and around it. Across the entrance is a grey stone tablet, its words almost worn away. So that the inscription will not be lost, a replica has recently been erected alongside the tunnel, with the original words:

The Kennet and Avon Canal Company
Inscribe this tunnel with the Name

BRUCE

In Testimony of their GRATITUDE
For the uniform and effectual support of
The Right honourable THOMAS BRUCE. EARL of AYLESBURY
and CHARLES LORD BRUCE. his Son
Through the whole Progress of this great National Work
By which a direct communication by Water was opened
Between the Cities of LONDON and BRISTOL
ANNO DOMINI 1810

The Earl of Ailesbury (not Aylesbury, as per the inscription) and his son both benefitted from the canal. They were able to ship out timber from Savernake Forest, and the pumping station at Crofton had a special pump to supply water to their house at nearby Tottenham Park.

Since the tunnel had to take Newbury Barges, it was larger than the narrow tunnels on many northern canals. Hence legging through it was not an option. Instead, there were chains, by which the boat was pulled through, while the horse went over the top. Charles Penruddocke, travelling

Top: The eastern portal of the Bruce Tunnel, with the newly erected replica inscription.

Above: The view from the fore-deck of a narrowboat as it leaves the tunnel, heading east. Modern boats have diesel engines, but the chains still exist along the southern wall for boats to be pulled through.

Opposite: Wilcot Wide Water, September 2009.

through in 1887, in his horse-drawn boat *Lucy*, described
how his guests fell silent and nothing was heard but the
subdued clanking of chains, once the tow-rope was cast
adrift and they were left to themselves and the darkness.
In 1928, CH Smith had an engine on his boat, but was
nervous about it breaking down in the tunnel. He called
it an uncanny experience, and explained how the engine
roared in the darkness, and how the sound died away when
the boat came out the other side. Even today, although the
tunnel is not long compared with some in the Midlands at
around 500yds (457m), the sound of the diesel engine seems
to pound along, and the escape from the tunnel is a relief.

For walkers, there is a short sharp climb and then a
level walk to the road, passing what was once the Savernake
station-master's house. The path then crosses towards an
elaborate bit of Victoriana, the former Savernake Forest
Hotel. It was built about 1864 by the Marquis of Ailesbury
for visitors arriving by train. It has recently been converted
to houses under the name Savernake Manor – even though

Left: The 'Private Fishing' sign
by the Great Western main
line.

Top right: Burbage Wharf in
September 1971.

Right: Burbage Wharf in 1982.

there has never been a manor of Savernake. The path goes beside the old hotel, and then, as you reach the railway line, there is a mystifying sign – 'Private Fishing'. It refers not to the railway, of course, but to the canal. The path dives down under the line, emerging just beyond the western portal of Bruce Tunnel.

The next point of interest is Burbage Wharf. Here, various goods, such as coal and bricks, and especially timber, were loaded or unloaded. The wooden crane was first erected in 1831. About 1973, the metal parts were retrieved and the crane rebuilt from locally sourced timber – but unfortunately not oak, which would have been very durable. Although it looked in good condition in 1982, it has deteriorated. Once again the metal parts have been rescued, and the crane rebuilt out of the oak for which the forest is famous.

Although much of this section, which includes the Fifteen Mile Pound, is flat, there is a short flight of four locks down to Wootton Rivers. The first is at Cadley Bridge, and, for the first time since leaving Reading, as we approach the head of the lock, a slow descent begins, towards Bristol.

Top: At Cadley Bridge the great descent towards Bristol has begun.

Above: Brimslade Farm buildings, erected after the canal had been built on the north side.

Left: The farmhouse, however, is on the south side and may go back to the sixteenth century.

Right: The lock at Wootton Rivers in the early 1900s, with a group of local inhabitants, young and old, keen to be in the photograph.

At Brimslade Bridge there are attractive brick-built farm buildings on the far side of the canal. These were built shortly after the K&A opened, presumably because the canal had divided Brimslade Farm House from some of its land. The house itself, which is certainly seventeenth century and may go back to the sixteenth century, can be seen on the right-hand side, as the towpath passes under the bridge.

A mile further on is Wootton Rivers. Until comparatively recently, the lock-keeper's cottage was still lived in by a lock-keeper – now it is a private house, and its roof is no longer thatched but tiled. Wootton Rivers consists of one long street, with houses, thatched and unthatched, along its length. The church clock is a curiosity, having the

Above: The *Charlotte Dundas* near Pewsey, April 1972.

Left: Pewsey Wharf looks deserted in this postcard from the 1920s.

words 'GLORY BE TO GOD' instead of numbers. It was made out of scrap metal by the local blacksmith, Jack Spratt, in 1911.

From now on, life is easier for boaters, as there are no locks and virtually no swing bridges – those shown on old maps have largely disappeared. However, for walkers it soon becomes apparent that locks have a pleasing tendency to measure progress, and the Fifteen Mile Pound can seem a long 15 miles. However, there are several points of interest.

The first, nearly three miles from Wootton Rivers, is Pewsey Wharf. With the restoration of the K&A, this is once again a busy place, with boats of all kinds moored up, not just the odd rowing boat. During the canal's long decline, it became quiet and derelict, its quays overgrown. Today, the warehouse is the Waterfront Inn, serving meals and real ale. There is also the French Horn, over the road, built as a row of cottages around 1830, which became an inn around 1855.

Pewsey itself is a mile and a half down the road – which may explain why the wharf became derelict once the railway arrived. It was quicker and easier for Pewsey people to use the station. In the days when the canal was the one way out for heavy goods, they would have been taken there by cart. It seems that some carters were cruel to their horses, as a sign was put up at the bottom of the hill, with a homily about mistreating animals. In 1982, the original sign was still there, but, following vandalism, a more durable replica has been erected.

As if to make up for the lack of locks, some of the bridges along this stretch are more interesting than the plain brick ones we have seen hitherto. For instance, about half a mile past Pewsey, the elegant Bristow Bridge appears among the trees. Walkers need to use this bridge as the towpath changes sides.

In 1982, the old sign at the bottom of the hill in Pewsey was still there.

By 2009 it had been replaced by something more vandal-proof.

As if to make up for the lack of locks, the bridges become more interesting. This is Bristow Bridge.

Dredge's bridge is seen beyond the lodge on this postcard from around 1910.

Shortly after this comes an unusual suspension bridge, now looking rather sad and sorry for itself. It was built by James Dredge of Bath. Although a brewer by trade, he designed what was in effect a double cantilever bridge, with the continuous deck supported by chains. He built around 50 of them, of which only a few survive. Perhaps the best example is Victoria Bridge in Bath, which will be encountered in Chapter 7. Dating from 1836, it was the first to be built. The bridge at Wilcot was commissioned by Colonel Wroughton of Stowell Park in 1845.

Two earlier members of the Wroughton family, the colonel's grandmother and aunt, both named Susannah, also had an effect on the landscaping of the canal. They were reluctant to allow the canal to cross their land, but finally agreed, under certain conditions. They insisted

Wilcot Wide Water with the Ladies Bridge in the distance.

The view eastwards over Wilcot Wide Water in snowy conditions.

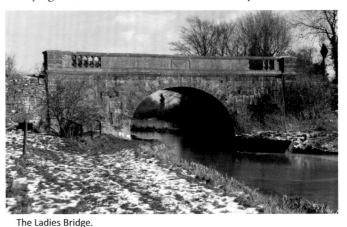

The Ladies Bridge.

A detail of the decoration.

This milepost was photographed near Ladies Bridge in April 1972.

Looking east along the canal near Alton Barnes, with Picked – or Pecked – Hill in the distance.

All that remains of the swing bridge at Lambpit Copse.

The large concrete cylinders flanking Woodborough Fields Bridge, designed to stop Hitler's tanks crossing the canal.

that the canal be widened out to make a landscape feature, with an ornamental bridge at the end. Although Wilcot Wide Water looks like a lake, the main stream of the canal hugs the northern side. In summer, it is a pleasant place to moor up, especially if your boat is a floating garden like that featured on page 60. Watch out for the heron who likes to fish here. As requested, the ladies got their bridge which is still known as the Ladies Bridge today. Although designed by John Rennie, the carving, especially of the swags, is somewhat crude. It has recently been completely restored.

Shortly after leaving Wilcot, we see, beside the path, a small building which recalls more recent history – World War II, when, as previously mentioned, the canal was planned as the first line of defence in the event of a German invasion. A little hut – a typical piece of MoD architecture – is rapidly acquiring some amusing decorations, and seems to have been christened Heaven's Waiting Room.

Above: Honeystreet, the home of Robbins, Lane & Pinniger, around 1910, with *Unity* moored up at the wharf.

Left: The Barge at Honeystreet, now being given a new role as a community pub after the project team won a Lottery Fund award to buy the lease.

Right: The Green Man on the ceiling of the room at the Barge Inn dedicated to crop circles.

Ashton C Allen's steam launch *Eva* beside the swing bridge at Allington around 1890. The Alton Barnes White Horse can be seen faintly on the hillside above the boy standing in the middle of the bridge. The cottage on the right has vanished, but older Ordnance Survey maps show a building on this site, which may have been called Canal Cottage. All that remains is a heap of rubble, and the neat hedge is now a row of straggly trees. Indeed, the whole of this view is now blocked by trees. Above the hedge one can just make out gothick-style windows. Several of the lock-keeper's and lengthsman's cottages at Bath have this pattern, so it seems likely that it was connected with the canal.

In a field a little further on is a strange survival – a remnant of Lambpit Swing Bridge. The bridge had gone by 1975, so it is extraordinary that the remains are still here. At Woodborough Fields Bridge there are more World War II defences, designed to stop tanks crossing the bridge.

Another mile brings us to Honeystreet – the home of Robbins, Lane & Pinniger, carriers and boat-builders, known as RL&P. They once owned most of the village. They were also responsible for making sure that the GWR kept to its obligations over the canal, and threatening it with legal action if it did not. It was they who converted an old narrowboat into what Charles Penruddocke called a houseboat and christened *Lucy* for his journey along the canal in 1887 – perhaps one of the earliest such conversions recorded. *Unity* was one of their best-known barges, and she was used to carry some of the materials for the construction of World War II defences along the canal. She also carried carboys of acid from Avonmouth back to Honeystreet for making fertilizer – another RL&P industry. The GWR refused to carry them on the grounds that they were a hazardous cargo.

Honeystreet Bridge carries a much older route – the Wessex Ridgeway. Also at Honeystreet is the legendary Barge Inn, built in 1810 as a canalside pub. Known in its heyday as the George, the establishment contained a slaughter house, coach house and stabling for four horses, as well as a brew house, hop store, bake house, smoke house and cart shed. The north section of the ground floor included a grocery and general stores, and between 1871 and 1957 a number of licensees also acted as local grocers.

Fire broke out on 14 December 1858, destroying the original building and leading to what the *Devizes & Wiltshire Gazette* referred to as a 'disgraceful scene. Soon after the fire was extinguished …… the cellars were entered …. and there was nothing but drunkenness and confusion.'

However, due to its importance, the Barge Inn was rebuilt in just six months, an event commemorated by a plaque on the gable end. The inn, which now had no fewer than 24 rooms in the main building, flourished, along with other industries here such as the sawmills, builder's wharf and coal stores.

Despite the canal's decline, the presence of RL&P at Honeystreet meant that the wharf continued to be a busy

Above: Horton Fields Bridge – a bridge no longer.

Left: The old weight restriction sign on Bishops Cannings Swing Bridge.

place. When the Barge Inn was sold by auction in 1897, it made £2,100 – a considerable sum then. The lease has just been sold again – this time to a village community group, who plan to run it. They achieved their goal when the project won a lottery grant. It is well known as a centre for crop-circle enthusiasts, and has some extraordinary paintings, including a Green Man, on the ceiling of one of the rooms.

Two and half miles on, the next swing bridge carries a footpath from All Cannings to Allington. Mrs Luffman, of All Cannings Women's Institute, narrates the story of a ghost which haunts this stretch of the K&A. He takes the form of a hobgoblin, and throws people into the canal at night. Since there is a pub at All Cannings and none at Allington, it seems more likely that this is a story dreamt up by drinkers from the latter village as they made their way home rather unsteadily.

After Allington Bridge, there is another swing bridge, but not one that need trouble the boater. Horton Fields Bridge lies on the bank, unused and rotting. Shortly after this, the vegetation on the banks can be over head height, and the walker only catches glimpses of passing boats. Near Horton, however, the view clears, and the tall spire of Bishops Cannings Church, said to emulate that of Salisbury Cathedral, can be seen in the distance. The church is well worth a visit, and there is a good pub, although another pub, the Bridge, is further along the towpath at Horton. A swing bridge carries a footpath to the village. Although this bridge is a restoration, it still carries the old warning sign.

The new marina at Devizes with the White Horse on Roundway Hill, cut by around 200 local people in 1999 to mark the millennium, in the distance.

An Edwardian postcard of the wooded cutting on the approach to Devizes. Eventually houses appear among the trees.

Restoring Devizes Wharf in December 1978. The revitalised wharf, lit by the rays of the setting sun.

When the Kennet & Avon Canal Trust was trying to persuade councils to invest in the restoration, one inducement offered was that it would bring new jobs to the area. Proof of this can be seen with the marinas that have sprung up, such as the new one at Devizes. On the hillside above it can be seen another addition to the landscape – the Millennium White Horse, perhaps one of the few millennium projects to be completed on time, perhaps because it was carried out by local people.

Approaching Devizes, the canal once again runs in a gloomy cutting, as it curves alongside the London Road. At first wooded, soon the gardens of houses come down to meet the canal. Despite the growth of new housing estates around Devizes, this part of town has changed little in a century.

From now on, brick gives way to Bath stone in many of the bridges. The canal makes a sharp right-hand turn, and continues in a shallow cutting. When the path diverges, walkers should take the lower path, which goes under another Bath stone bridge, and finally leads to the Wharf. Formerly called Town Wharf, it is the only surviving wharf of three that once existed. The long building at right angles to the canal, originally a bonded warehouse, is the home of the Kennet & Avon Canal Trust, and houses its museum, while the quayside warehouse has been converted to a theatre.

Devizes is well worth exploring, and boaters will definitely want to take a break while they gather their energies for the hard work waiting for them beyond the wharf. Its streets have fascinating names such as The Brittox and Monday Market Street, while St John's Church has a very fine Norman interior. The Wiltshire Heritage Museum is also worth a visit. On a more practical level, there are several splendid old pubs, and Devizes is also the headquarters of Wadworth's, whose brewery dominates this end of town.

The market place shows how the canal changed the face of building in the town. The Bear Inn extends over two adjoining buildings, one built before the canal came, of brick, and the other after it arrived, of Bath stone. The Corn Exchange, built on the site of the inn's Assembly Rooms in 1857, is also of Bath stone.

In 1773, the landlord of the Bear was Thomas Lawrence, whose son, also called Thomas, would entertain guests by either reciting for them or drawing their portraits. Six years later, the elder Thomas's business failed, and the young Thomas became the family's money-earner thanks to his skill as an artist. From these humble beginnings came the man who in 1815 was knighted and later became President of the Royal Academy.

The market cross was erected in 1814 to replace an earlier one. On one of the panels are inscribed these words:

The Mayor and Corporation of Devizes avail themselves of the stability of this building to transmit to future times the record of an awful event which occurred in this market place in the year 1753 hoping that such record may serve as a salutary warning against the Danger of impiously invoking Devine Vengeance or of calling on the Holy Name of God to conceal the devices of falsehood and fraud.

On Thursday the twenty fifth day of January 1753 Ruth Pierce of Potterne in this County of Wiltshire agreed with three other women to buy a sack of wheat in the Market, each paying her due proportion towards the same. One of these women in collecting the several quotas of money discovered a deficiency in the total and demanded of Ruth Pierce the sum which was wanting to make good this amount. Ruth Pierce protested that she had paid her share and said she wished she might drop down dead if she had not. She rashly repeated this Awful wish when to the consternation and horror of the surrounding multitude she instantly fell down and expired having the money concealed in her hand.

On that sobering thought, it is perhaps time to return to the canal.

6 Devizes to Bath: Down to the Avon

In the 53 miles between Reading and Devizes, there are 57 locks – roughly a lock per mile. All that is about to change. In the remaining 34 miles, there are 50 locks, 29 of them spread over the next two miles. This is hard work for boaters, and to add to their problems there are shorter flights at Seend and Bath, and six swing bridges between Sells Green and Semington. It is payback time for the easy ride along the Fifteen Mile Pound. Walkers, on the other hand, now have plenty to look at and it's downhill all the way from here.

This enormous drop over such a short distance was not in the original plans. The route as first mooted would have gone via Marlborough, before coming down through Wiltshire via Lacock and Melksham. However, when Rennie conducted a survey, he concluded that the water supply along the proposed route would be inadequate. In addition, the two Devizes MPs had been lobbying for the canal to come via their town. And so, despite the obstacle of Caen Hill, that was the route chosen. In the end, the 29 locks in the flight – 16 of them in just over half a mile – took nearly ten years to build and this was the last part of the canal to be opened. However, while construction took place, a tramway was built which ran downhill from Devizes Wharf to Foxhangers. This accounts for the width of the path today. Goods from east or west would be transhipped on to the tramway at one end and back on to waiting boats at the other end.

The Devizes flight begins immediately on leaving the wharf – walkers, by the way, will find the towpath has changed sides. The first lock comes before Town Bridge, which walkers have to use as the towpath changes sides once more. However, they should not cross the road, but take the ramp on the same side of the road, which leads to a tunnel. This allowed the tramway to come up to the wharf. During World War I, the flight was used for training soldiers to operate canal locks.

At first the locks are spaced out quite gently, like a normal flight. A variety of boats have moorings in this stretch, both above and below Prison Bridge. In September 2009 they included a replica *Unity*, a very pink *Pink Panther*, and an old

Top: Soldiers training on the canal at Devizes during World War I. The tunnel through which the horse has just come was built for the tramway from Devizes Wharf to Foxhangers.

Above: The canal at Devizes around 1910.

Opposite: Caen Hill Flight, Devizes, c1890.

Above: Boats at Devizes, September 2009.

Below: The top of the Caen Hill flight around 1910.

Fellows, Morton & Clayton boat, still with her tarpaulin. At last one reaches the crest of the hill, and the ground drops away, to reveal a spectacular view. The lock-keeper's cottage is still there, but is now the Caen Hill Café.

Now comes the 16-lock flight. As one lock follows immediately on the next, there were going to be problems with water supply, so Rennie came up with the idea of building side pounds, which stretch across the hillside, acting as reservoirs for each lock.

At the bottom of the 16 locks, where the ground drops away, was a brickyard owned by the

A view down the flight, showing the side pounds, around 1910.

canal company, where the bricks for locks and bridges, as well as Bruce Tunnel, were made. The clay pit was discovered when work on the canal began and the works continued in production until 1961.

As late as 1928, CH Smith negotiated the locks without too much trouble. Just over 30 years later, the locks were derelict and de-gated, but today, after much hard work – including raising money and generating interest in restoration – boats can once again use this flight.

The flight is now supplied with water by back pumps, built at Foxhangers Wharf. After the canal reopened in 1990, but before the pumps were working, boats had to travel up or down in convoy on two days of the week. At about 9am there would be great excitement and jostling as boats which wanted to get away as soon as possible tried to rush up to the front, while the crews of boats who had been happily moored, as they thought, in pole position, got angry and flustered – all very entertaining to those who didn't mind what time they got away, as long as they got there in the end. Incidentally, Wikipedia says it takes five to six hours, but two experienced crews together can do it in four.

Charles Penruddocke said he did the 29 locks in three and a half hours – so perhaps having a horse made a difference.

Foxhangers Wharf is now the home of Foxhangers Canal Holidays, with their fleet of hire-boats all with foxy names. Beyond the wharf can be seen the remains of a bridge which carried the railway line from Devizes to Holt. A more spectacular bridge, which carried the same railway over the road which came down Caen Hill, parallel with the canal, and known as Fish Bridge, was demolished in 1968 to allow the road to be widened.

After going under two road bridges, we embark on a section with several swing bridges. There is also a flight of five locks, which begins at Seend Top Lock. Shortly after passing Seend Top Lock and going under a road bridge, it will be noticed that the field on the far side is rather lumpy, with a ramp running down to the canal. Incredible though it may seem in this peaceful spot, this was the site of an ironworks, which, had it not been for bad planning and greedy investors seeking a quick buck, might have turned this village into an industrial centre.

Above: Looking up the abandoned flight in 1982. Compare this with the photograph on page 74, taken in the 1890s, and the same view today, on the right.

The scrum at Foxhangers in 1994, when the Devizes flight was only open twice a week. At the time, the bridge in the background was in poor condition, with a massive crack. It has now been fully restored, which, since the towpath changes sides here once again, is very good news.

Foxhangers Wharf today, with the remains of the railway bridge beyond it.

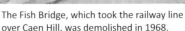

The Fish Bridge, which took the railway line over Caen Hill, was demolished in 1968.

Seend Top Lock

In the seventeenth century, John Aubrey found that the area was rich in iron. He had discovered it in the springs which he was keen to develop as a spa. He relates how he found iron ore after a rainstorm caused the iron in the stone to twinkle. He took the ore to Mr Newton, a local smith turned clock and fiddle-maker – 'an ingeniose man' – who assured him that he had smelted the ore in his forge. Aubrey realised, however, that the lack of fuel ruled out smelting on the site. Two centuries later, it was a different story, for the canal had been built. Not only could coal be brought in; iron could also be taken out.

Initially, ore was shipped out to Bristol before being sent to Wales for smelting. However, from 1857 onwards, attempts were made to smelt at Seend. Despite furnaces and a tramway being built, and even a railway siding from the works to the main line, by 1886 the works were described as derelict. Three years later the blast furnaces were demolished. Yet the iron had been of high quality. Some of the troubles were due to lack of finance, but others were due to shady dealing by the owners.

When Charles Penruddocke dropped off his passenger, Helen – almost certainly his niece – at Seend where she lived, the ruined smelters were still standing in this field. Mining continued sporadically until 1946, when it finally ceased. Today, the only relic of this failed enterprise, apart from the few humps and bumps in the field, the name of Rusty Lane and a house called Ferrum Towers, is the line of the siding which crossed the canal on a girder bridge, just before the road bridge, and which can still be discerned heading for the old railway line from Holt to Devizes.

Just beyond the bridge, on the far side of the canal, is the Barge Inn, which has been greatly extended since the early 1900s. It was opened as a beerhouse by 1857, and the owner seems to have been a beer retailer, coal merchant, baker and grocer, with his livelihood coming from the canal community. The same could be said today, since it is now a family-friendly food pub. Lovers of more traditional pubs may prefer to make the 200 yard (180 metre) trek up the hill to the Brewery, a pub converted from two cottages in the mid-nineteenth century.

The canal goes past Seend Park Farm, home of local business man and rally driver Freddie Giles. Watch out for his extraordinary collection of all sorts of advertising material. He has also built himself a tithe barn – a wonderful timbered building, which despite its venerable appearance is quite new. Meanwhile, his neighbours at Melksham Park Farm have good news for boaters. They have removed swing bridge No 157, converting its site to their private picnic spot.

Seend Ironworks in the 1870s. The canal passed under the road bridge in the foreground, which is still there today. The girder bridge beyond it, however, which was built over Seend Middle Lock, is long gone.

Top: The sunlit house on this Edwardian postcard is the Barge Inn. The ironworks had been demolished several years earlier, but the bridge on the left is the one in the photograph on the previous page.

Centre: The Barge Inn can also be seen in the photograph below, taken in December 1978, when the lock was being restored.

Bottom: The Barge Inn today.

All along the canal, there is plenty of wildlife, yet some are concerned it will be deterred by human activity. All these people and boats, they maintain, will destroy the natural habitat. First of all, a canal is not a natural habitat – it is man-made – but if, thanks to dereliction, it has become a wild place, there may be a conflict. Wildlife, however, is surprisingly resilient. A kingfisher is frequently seen flying up and down near a busy road in Bath, past a row of moored boats, unnoticed by crowds of people on the towpath. Here, just beyond the lock at Seend, is another example. These pictures were taken on a day when there were plenty of boats about, close to the busy Barge Inn. A heron uses the gangplank of a narrowboat as a convenient fishing station and is so intent on what he is doing that he is oblivious to the photographer standing so close that his reflection can be seen in one of the pictures.

Top left: The New Semington aqueduct, opened in March 2004.

Above left: Semington Junction, where the Wilts and Berks left the K&A, seen here around 1900. The man on the boat seems to be trying to manoeuvre away from it. The house up on the lock is still there.

Top right: The first of the Bath Stone aqueducts is at Semington. It is now in a poor state of repair, and largely patched with GWR engineering brick.

Centre right: The Somerset Arms at Semington.

Bottom right: A barge carrying a school party appears unexpectedly out of the mist on a wet and windy day in 1982.

Some changes to the canal are very recent, including a new aqueduct over the A350 Semington Bypass. It was opened in March 2004 by Fleur de Rhé-Philippe. She was the Cabinet Member for the Environment in what was then still known as Wiltshire County Council, but to K&A Trust members she was better known as the company secretary of the Trust for 15 years. She was also instrumental in securing a £25 million lottery grant towards its restoration.

Immediately below the second lock at Semington, the towpath swerves and there are some strange-looking railings. They are made of fish-belly rail from the Avon & Gloucestershire Railway, which ran from the Bristol coalfields down to the River Avon, and was owned by the K&ACC. They are here because this was once a bridge over the Wilts & Berks Canal. Chapter 10 gives you some more information on this canal, but in the meantime look over the hedge into the garden of the house on the other side. This was the toll-collector's house, and the regulating lock, which controlled the flow of water between the two canals, is now buried beneath the garden. The junction is closed off by a wall of concrete blocks.

Boats can be hired from Tranquil Boats at Semington, and anyone needing refreshment will find it at the excellent Somerset Arms in Semington, by taking the road over the bridge and heading south for about 500 yards (450 metres).

Just beyond the locks, there is a stretch of Bath stone wall beside the towpath. This is Semington Aqueduct – now almost invisible from the canal, although fortunately this was not the case when the photograph on the left was taken in 1982.

The canal now wanders through some strange and seemingly remote countryside – it is hard to believe that there are several busy towns not far away. In 1982, it seemed so lonely and remote that when a barge carrying an excited group of small children on a school outing suddenly appeared by Semington Swing Bridge, it was noteworthy

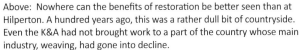

Above: Nowhere can the benefits of restoration be better seen than at Hilperton. A hundred years ago, this was a rather dull bit of countryside. Even the K&A had not brought work to a part of the country whose main industry, weaving, had gone into decline.

Below & right: Today at Hilperton the old bridge which crossed the canal, just visible in the picture above, has been turned through 90° to form the entrance to a marina, around which new homes have been built. A busy boatyard provides a service for travellers. It is a pity that the replacement bridge, built to cope with the increase in traffic, had to be so utilitarian.

enough to photograph it. Today, that same spot has several narrowboats moored up, and the towpath, just a grassy walkway in 1982, is now well-worn.

The changes wrought since 1990, when the canal reopened, further manifest themselves at Hilperton, where there is a marina, new houses and a busy boatyard. The canal was intended to go through Trowbridge, but to save extra engineering work, including a large aqueduct, the nearest it got to the town was Hilperton. However, an aqueduct was needed here over the River Biss. Like the Semington Aqueduct, it is now almost impossible to see from the canal, but in 1982 it was possible to scramble down and take a photograph. Since it is a very fine piece of architecture, it is a pity it is not more visible. The same could be said of the Ladydown Aqueduct, which is crossed, almost unnoticed, just before reaching the Biss Aqueduct. It was built by IK Brunel around 1848 to carry the canal over the GWR line from Thingley Junction to Westbury.

After a mile and a half of pleasant walking along the tree-lined path, we reach the outskirts of Bradford on Avon. On the far side of the canal is the Bradford on Avon Marina. Then comes a bridge. Here you could once have refreshed yourself at the Beehive, but it has been killed off – a victim of bad management, lack of vision and a council prepared to ignore local wishes. Soon Bradford Wharf comes into view. It is now a busy destination, as you will have guessed from the number of moored boats you have already passed. The K&A Trust has a shop and tearoom here in the old lock-keeper's cottage, while on the other side of the canal is the Barge Inn.

Among the other buildings that have survived is an impressive wharfinger's house. The lock just before the bridge was, when first built, the deepest on the canal. Beside it is the old wharf warehouse and the only operational gauging dry dock of its kind in the country. The Kennet & Avon Canal Company used it to check the carrying capacity of barges and so calculate tolls.

Ladydown Aqueduct, built in 1848 when the GWR line from Thingley Junction to Westbury opened, and the only aqueduct on the canal designed by IK Brunel.

The next aqueduct, by Rennie, is the rather fine Biss Aqueduct – unfortunately now almost inaccessible to curious onlookers.

The Beehive at Bradford on Avon in September 2009.

Bradford Wharf (above), with the gauging dock (below), here seen with the former K&A Trust boat, *Ladywood*, being given some maintenance. She was decommissioned in 1999 and replaced by a purpose-built wide-beamed boat, with a lift for wheelchair access. It is called the *Barbara McLellan*, after the lady who set up the charitable trust which enabled the K&A Trust to buy it.

The towpath continues on the other side of the road, past what was once the Lower Wharf, where you will find the Canal Inn and the Lock Inn Café. Bradford on Avon, which lies off to the right, is well worth exploring, with such attractions as a Saxon Church, weavers' houses, steep alleys and an old bridge with a lock-up. High on a hill is the little chapel of St Mary Tory, while down near the river is the magnificent Church of the Holy Trinity. Old mills, such as Abbey Mills, stand as monuments to the once thriving wool trade, though most are now converted to housing. As we continue along the canal, we pass a fourteenth-century Tithe Barn and Barton Farm, which originally belonged to the nuns of Shaftesbury Abbey.

Bradford on Avon is, perhaps surprisingly for a small market town, of interest to people keen on the history of transport. It is the home of the Moulton bicycle, invented by Alex Moulton, who also designed the suspension system for the Mini. He was the grandson of Stephen Moulton, a pioneer in the use of rubber, who converted two old woollen mills in Bradford on Avon to factories. The railway station

was designed by Brunel, while a reminder of an earlier form of transport comes in the form of a fourteenth-century packhorse bridge.

We continue along the hillside above Barton Farm Country Park. This section caused many problems, as the underlying

Top left: The canal passes fourteenth-century Barton Farm, with its fine Tithe Barn.

Centre left: Also dating from the fourteenth century is the packhorse bridge – a reminder of what the canal replaced. This photograph by Ashton C Allen shows the corner of the Tithe Barn and the canal embankment, just visible above the bridge.

Bottom left: At Avoncliff, the canal makes a sharp right turn to cross the Avon.

Below: Avoncliff Aqueduct developed the slight sag in the centre arch early on, but it never worsened, and the aqueduct still stands. It is seen here in 1971.

Bottom: Wounded soldiers on *Bittern* during World War I.

Above: On this postcard of Avoncliff from around 1904 we can see an old mill chimney, the Cross Guns Inn, the houses by the canal, and the aqueduct. A tramway ran across the aqueduct where the towpath now runs. After the railway opened in 1857, this brought stone from the Westwood quarries across the aqueduct and down to a siding beside the line. In the foreground, the first bit of the aqueduct is a later addition, constructed when the railway was built.

Right: By the time this postcard was published around 1910, the tramway had gone. An engine can be seen on the GWR line, however, with stone piled up by the sidings. The larger-than-life swans appear on many cards by this publisher, R Wilkinson of Trowbridge.

Before restoration this section of the canal was dewatered due to serious leakages. The bed had to be relined throughout before water could be reintroduced. This is the view of Avoncliiff Aqueduct from the south in May 1971.

Top: Avoncliff Aqueduct in January 1980 before restoration started in earnest.

Above: The same view in April 1980 with work well advanced.

Top right: Both techniques used to line the canal can be seen here: in the foreground, traditional clay-puddling; beyond it, the new concrete lining put in to prevent the landslips and breaches to which this section had always been prone.

Centre right: On this 1920s postcard, a boy stands fishing by a pair of stop gates.

Bottom right: A closer view of the gates.

strata is that fine clay known as Fuller's Earth. To combat this, Rennie built a series of drains under the canal, to take excess water away without damaging the canal. This scheme has not always been successful and the drains themselves have caused problems, but by and large they have done the job for which they were designed, because the canal is still here.

Just over a mile further on, the canal does a sharp right turn, to cross the most spectacular aqueduct so far, at Avoncliff. Look out for the stone pillar, with the grooves cut into it by the towing ropes, as the horses turned while the boat was still back down the cut. This is called a towing post, and was designed to prevent damage to property.

Avoncliff Aqueduct carries the canal from one side of the Avon valley to the other. There are three arches. The central one has a pronounced sag, which developed almost immediately after the aqueduct was built, and has not worsened since. The towpath changes sides here, and you have to head towards the Cross Guns Inn, which you might wish to visit before continuing on your way. Not only is it very old – dating back to the early seventeenth century, and possibly earlier – but it is also the brewery tap for Box Steam Brewery. To pick up the towpath again, head under the aqueduct and come up on the other side.

Having regained the towpath, take a good look around. Avoncliff was once an industrial centre, with several mills. Looking up the River Avon, the old mill by the weir is currently being restored, while the mill at the other end of the weir, below the Cross Guns, is a private house. Downstream, looking over to the left, you may catch a glimpse of Ancliff Square – originally weavers' accommodation, then a mill and then, when the wool trade went into decline, a workhouse. It later became an hotel, was subsequently converted into flats and finally reconverted into twelve houses. Avoncliff has its own very interesting website at *www.avoncliff.co.uk*.

During World War I, the workhouse was converted to a convalescent hospital for wounded soldiers. They were taken into Bradford on Avon in the Red Cross barge, *Bittern*. Many pub landlords supplied the soldiers with free beer, so the nurses were required to help the soldiers back to the hospital, sometimes even having to come to the basin with stretchers. It is fortunate that the nurses were sympathetic!

The next section of the canal, from Avoncliff to Limpley Stoke, was known as the dry section due to its propensity to leak and have slippages. In the late 1970s, it was decided to do away with the traditional, clay-puddled bottom to the canal, and substitute a sandwich made up of sheeting, hardcore, more sheeting and finally reinforced concrete. This change takes place just beyond the western end of the aqueduct.

Shortly after leaving the aqueduct, look out for a post with a wooden sign on it – '67 II'. This is a quarter mile post, put up by the GWR and made from an old piece of railway line. It indicates that you are 67½ miles from Reading.

This section winds its way around the wooded hillside, and is a peaceful shady place in summer. At various points along this stretch you will notice recesses for gates. They are not locks but stop-gates. These were installed so that if there was a breach – as happened all too often along here – the loosely-hinged gates at each end of the affected section would swing closed, thereby preventing loss of water and limiting the amount of flood damage. British Waterways has now placed so much faith in their rigid lining that the gates, which were still there until recently, have been removed. Everyone is hoping that their faith is not misplaced.

There is also a lengthman's cottage along here. Lengths-men played an important role on a section so prone to problems. They checked the banks for damage, including signs of animals burrowing into them. We may like to see water-voles, but back then they were considered persona

Top left: An historic picture, showing the concrete lining being put in, the gate recesses for a double pair of stop gates, and the lengthman's cottage. Today, this cottage has an extra floor and manicured gardens.

Bottom left: The K&A follows the 54m (177ft) contour line and some idea of what that means can be seen in this postcard view from the 1920s, with the canal crossing the centre of the picture. The canal has to cross the valley again before reaching Bath. Note the small house between two trees alongside the canal in the centre of the picture.

Top right: Here is the view from the canal, looking towards the hillside where the previous photograph was taken. This 1930s photograph was taken from the bridge, and the small house in the previous photograph can be seen in the foreground.

Bottom right: The same stretch of canal in July 1978, with restoration under way.

non grata. Today, however, canals are regarded as one of the principal habitats of this endangered species. There was a double set of stop-gates in front of the cottage, which makes sense, as the lengthsman would see if there was trouble in either direction immediately on coming out of his house.

It was also somewhere along this stretch that work started on building the canal. The *Bath Chronicle* of 27 November 1794 reported that on 'Wednesday the 12th instant, some of the contractors for the Kennet & Avon Canal began their work in the parish of Winsley, between Freshford and this city'.

The canal passes high above the village of Limpley Stoke, which can be seen on your left. Its history is linked with Saxon kings, including Alfred and the first man to be crowned king of all England, Edgar. It was Edgar's daughter Edith who was patroness of the church.

In this view from around 1900 two horses have rounded the corner and are about to cross Dundas Aqueduct. The boat is still out of sight but the use of two horses suggests the load is heavy – probably stone.

The canal then makes a sharp left turn to approach the final aqueduct, the most magnificent structure on the canal. This is the Dundas Aqueduct, named after Charles Dundas, first chairman of the K&ACC. A tramway from the quarries at Conkwell came down to the canal – its line can still just be made out by the Monkton Combe School boathouse. The stone was intended for use in the construction of the canal, but it was of poor quality and quarrying stopped.

Two metal posts here prevent towropes from cutting the corner. Despite being of cast iron, the ropes have cut deeply into them.

On the other side of the aqueduct is Dundas Basin, with a crane – cast-iron this time, not wooden like that at Burbage Wharf – and a warehouse. There is also an aluminium bridge which leads into what are now moorings. This was the entrance to the Somersetshire Coal Canal. The lock at the entrance was a regulating lock like that at the entrance to the Wilts & Berks Canal at Semington. We will look at the Somersetshire Coal Canal in Chapter 9.

There is something of a mystery over the footbridge which carries the towpath to the south side of the canal. In his book, *The Kennet & Avon Canal – A Journey from Newbury to Bath in 1964*, John Russell is adamant that there has always a wooden bridge here, looking much as it does today. However, an engraving accompanying an advertisement for the Scotch Boat shows an arched bridge at this point. An early photograph confirms that this was not mere artistic licence. If you look at the bridge carefully, you can see that the string course meets a slight recess. On the north side the coping stones have been raised to make it level, but on the south side, they remain arched. When the stone bridge was replaced by a wooden one, however, remains a mystery – so far.

The grandest of all Rennie's structures on the canal – the Dundas Aqueduct. This illustration by JC Nattes shows it when it was new, in 1804. It also shows the quarry tramway coming down the hillside from the Conkwell quarries, and a sailing boat about to cross.

PACKER & KIVER,
(Late Parker,)
CLAVERTON HOTEL, DUNDAS AQUEDUCT, NEAR BATH.
The Scenery of which is most beautiful & not surpassed in the West of England.
WINES, SPIRITS & REFRESHMENT OF THE BEST QUALITY ON REASONABLE TERMS.

This engraving, dating from the 1840s, shows the aqueduct from the east. Despite its slightly amateurish look, this is a very accurate picture. On the far side of the aqueduct, we can see the bridge, drawn with a very pronounced arch, over the Somersetshire Coal Canal, which joined the K&A at Dundas Basin, The other bridge on the far side carried the towpath from one side of the canal to the other. It can be seen that, unlike the bridge that is there today, it has an arch. The boat just disappearing out of the picture is the Scotch Boat, advertised by the owners of the hotel on the hillside as 'celebrated' and 'swift sailing'. One of the reasons for its swiftness was the speed of the horses, which can be seen galloping along, urged on by the enthusiastic postilion on the second horse.

The mystery of the footbridge at Dundas Basin. The photograph on the left, taken around 1900, shows the bridge as we know it today, but the one on the right, taken some years earlier, confirms the evidence of the engraving above – that originally this was a normal bridge with a stone arch.

DUNDAS   LIMPLEYSTOKE

PACKER & KIVER'S
(Late Parkers)
Celebrated and Swift Sailing
Scotch Boat,

Leaves *BRADFORD* at ½ past 8 Morning & 4 in the Afternoon
and *BATH* at 11 in the Morning & 5 in the Evening (Abbey time)
From 1st April to the end of September

and from *BRADFORD* at 9 in the morning & 3 in the Afternoon
and *BATH* at 11 in the morning & 5 in the Evening (Abbey time)
From 1st October to the end of March

also *Pleasure Boats* at 3 o'clock Afternoon from *BATH*
to *CLAVERTON HOTEL* and *Neighbourhood,* and return at
7 o'clock in the evening

SUNDAYS EXCEPTED.

an *Omnibus* from *Bradford to Trowbridge* on arrival
of the *Boat.*
The *Boat* arrives in *Bath* in time for the *Great Western Railway*

Above: Cows grazing at Dundas Basin. The warehouse and the crane on the wharf are both still there today. It can be seen how hump-backed the bridge at the entrance of the coal canal was – and how accurate the engraving on the previous page was.

Right: A reminder of busier times – an advertisement for the Celebrated Scotch Boat from the 1840s.

As at Avoncliff, when the railway came an extra aqueduct had to be added at Dundas. On the left the double aqueduct is seen from the west. Below, seen from across the river, a Bath-bound train heads towards the canal around 1910.

Above: Looking east across the aqueduct in the 1890s, with the canal basin in the foreground and the entrance to the Coal Canal on the right.

Right: Looking east across the aqueduct in February 1984 as restoration gets under way.

Above: Looking west across Dundas Aqueduct during World War I as a boatload of recuperating soldiers attracts a small crowd.

Left: Looking west across the aqueduct in June 1984 after the concrete lining had been installed.

Right: A party from Bath's Trim Street Chapel set off from Dundas Basin for a picnic in 1901.

Below: *Viceroy* leads the reopening procession at Easter 1982.

Left: One of the winches in March 1973.

Below: Heritage Lottery funding paid for a new lining to be laid all the way into Bath. So far, it has proved successful.

Right: Claverton Pumping Station in May 1971.

During restoration work, the aqueduct remained a problem, since it leaked. However, it was successfully dammed off, and at Easter 1982 the canal reopened from Bath to Dundas Basin, with a procession from Bathampton led by the Fellows, Morton & Clayton steamer *Viceroy*. It was a joyful day for everyone at the Bath end – at long last progress was visible.

As you walk along here, you may spot small pieces of winding gear beside the path. At one time you would have seen chains leading from them into the canal, particularly along the Limpley Stoke stretch. These were attached to plugs in the canal bed. At certain places, especially near bridges, you will notice slots in the stone work. These can be used to make a dam by lowering planks, known as stop planks, into them. Then, when a section is dammed off at each end, the plug can be pulled so that water drains away through sluices into the river.

When you reach Claverton Bridge, it is worth checking if Claverton Pumping Station is open. In order to supply a good head of water to the flight of locks at Bath, an old mill was purchased from the Duke of Somerset and converted to a pumping station, a purpose-built pump-house being added, to Rennie's design. The breast-shot waterwheel drives the pumps. In effect, the river is pumping itself – a supremely elegant solution. Like Crofton, it was restored by a band of volunteers, who also maintain it. In its picturesque setting, it is well worth a visit.

Across the valley is Warleigh Manor, built in 1815 by Henry Skrine, whose family had owned the manor since the seventeenth century, and regarded as a very early example of the Tudor Revival. In 1956, the last of the Skrine family died and it was sold. After having been a variety of

educational establishments, including a reform school, it has now been converted to flats.

The next swing bridge is at Hampton Wharf. A tramway, which ran down to it from quarries on Bathampton Down, can still be followed – a footpath goes over the bridge, to the left and then up the hillside, where stone sleepers can be seen in the grass. The tramway used to cross the road on a bridge called the Dry Arch, but this was demolished in the 1970s. Today, anyone following the course of the tramway must, on reaching the road, turn right and then cross opposite what looks like a driveway, to rejoin the path on the other side. It then climbs steeply to the quarries which are now part of the National Trust's Skyline Walk. It is worth making this expedition to discover

Above: Hampton Wharf in the early twentieth century. Years of neglect are evident from the weed growing on the surface of the water. .

Below: Hampton Wharf in May 1971, with the triumph of nature epitomised by the swan sitting undisturbed on its nest amid the reed-choked waterway.

Right: The line of the old tramway running down to Hampton Wharf.

how steep a tramway could be, and to see the relics of an industry that was so vital to the canal.

Hampton Wharf was for many years the home of Sir John Knill, who, along with John Gould, began using the canal to transport goods after World War II. Since the British Transport Commission planned to close the canal on the grounds that it was defunct, businesses using the canal were not what it wanted to see. The BTC was therefore provoked into action to prevent them from continuing.

However, in their haste to stop them, unwise and illegal decisions were made, and enough time was gained and enough indignation generated to get the opposition going. The Knill family still maintains a presence here, including running the *Lady Lena*, built in 1890 and possibly the oldest electric launch in existence.

The views from the canal here across the valley towards Bathford are impressive, but eventually the canal makes another, gentler, left turn and arrives at Bathampton, where

FROM DRY ARCH, BATH.

Left: The Dry Arch carried the tramway over the Warminster Road. When this postcard was published in the early 1900s, the road had changed little since the Bath & Warminster Turnpike Trust built it in 1834. Today, it is the busy A36. The canal, deserted apart from a few walkers, can be seen on the left.

Below left: A photograph taken from the Dry Arch in May 1971, shortly before it was demolished. The road is out of shot to the right, and the railway and river can be seen on the far side of the canal. The canal bed is dry, with only a few pools of water to indicate what it once was. How many people, confronted by scenes like this, believed it would ever reopen?

Below: A horse tows one of the last working boats along the canal near Bathampton.

Bottom: The *Lady Lena*.

Above: Walking on the frozen canal at Bathampton in 1925. Harbutt's Mill, where Plasticine was made, is in the background.

Left: Maintenance work at Bathampton in the early twentieth century, probably to repair one of the culverts Rennie built under the canal to drain water from higher ground.

Below: Bathampton in the mid 1960s, showing the mill built after the fire in 1963. In the mid 1960s the towpath was narrow and grass-lined. Walkers were rarely seen although the *Charlotte Dundas*, a trip-boat built out of an old dredger by Lt-Cmdr Wray-Bliss, could sail up as far as here.

Opposite page: The procession prepares to leave Bathampton for Dundas on Easter Saturday, 1982.

it was originally planned to join the River Avon, until the route was changed, and the K&ACC pressed on to Bath. So successful has the restoration been in bringing back people to the canal that today this stretch is permanently lined with moored boats.

Bathampton has long been a favourite spot for photographers. Harbutt's Mill, where Plasticine was made, dominates many old views of the canal. Many of the Harbutt family, who lived nearby, were keen photographers and some of their views from the early twentieth century are seen here.

The canal passes the village school and the Church of St Nicholas. This dates from the fourteenth century, and has an Australian Chapel, dedicated to Arthur Phillip, first governor of New South Wales. In the churchyard are the graves of Walter Sickert, his wife Therese Lessore, and Vicomte Jean Baptiste du Barry, killed in a duel on Bathampton Down.

In 1963, the old Harbutt's Mill burnt down, and was replaced by a modern building. The factory finally closed in 1983, and there are now retirement homes on the site.

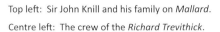

Top left: Sir John Knill and his family on *Mallard*.

Centre left: The crew of the *Richard Trevithick*.

Bottom left: The smartly turned out crew of the *Border Gypsy*.

Below: Another picture taken in the hard winter of 1925.

Bottom: Folly Footbridge – now replaced by a wooden up and over bridge.

In 1982, on an overcast Easter Saturday, boats lined up for the historic trip to Dundas Basin – a commonplace trip today, but a memorable occasion then. In the procession were Sir John Knill and his family on *Mallard*, the crew of *NB Richard Trevithick*, and the smartly turned out crew of *NB Border Gypsy*, who had had an epic journey to get here. Slowly the procession made its way along the hillside. It would be another eight years before the canal completely reopened.

Dredging has always been a necessary part of canal maintenance. Here is a dredger at work in the 1920s, just west of Folly Footbridge.

Three people on Folly Footbridge on a windy day. Were they on their way to the Folly public house – or just going for a walk?

The towpath continues west with gardens on the left, and the GWR main line and the River Avon on the right. The next swing bridge was the Folly Footbridge, named after a pub that stood at the bottom of a flight of steps leading from the towpath. The pub even had its own brewery. It suffered damage in a bombing raid in World War II, but could have been repaired. However, by that time it was so run down it was not worth saving. Thanks to persistent vandalism, the swing bridge has been replaced with a fixed 'up and over' bridge.

On the other side, the path climbs steeply up through a field which, despite the spread of modern housing elsewhere in Bath, remains open today. Sheep still graze here. Just west of it, however, are some Admiralty hutments dating from World War II. At the time of writing, the future of these is under consideration, and housing may be built on the site.

As the canal neared Bath, it followed the contour line round in a great sweep. However, when Brunel brought the GWR to Bath, he eventually decided to build the railway on the line of the canal, albeit at a lower level, after rejecting his original idea to take it to the north of Hampton Row. This meant rerouting the canal – which the GWR did not then own – cutting a slice out of the hillside and building a huge wall to shore up the canal in its new bed. Looking along the line of the rerouting, it can be appreciated what an astonishing feat of engineering this was. The trees on the

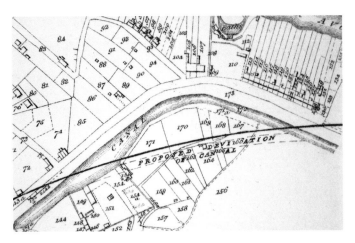

Above: Brunel's plan for the rerouting of the canal.

Left: The Humane Society's sign at Darlington Wharf.

Below: Darlington Wharf in the mid-nineteenth century.

Above right: Dredging at Darlington Wharf in May 1976.

north side of the railway are where the canal bank once was, and in Beckford Gardens, the street running alongside and above the line, there is a cottage that may once have been associated with the canal. Hampton Row, to the east, once faced directly out on to the canal embankment, not on to the railway line as it does today. A railway halt opened here in 1907, but closed ten years later.

Just beyond this was Darlington Wharf, where passengers picked up the Scotch Boats we have already met at Dundas Aqueduct. They were known as Scotch Boats because packet or passenger boats of this kind were based on a prototype originally found on the Monkland Canal, which ran from Glasgow to Woodhall. It was standard practice for them to be hauled by two horses, the second ridden by a postilion, as shown in the engraving on page 93. Express passenger boats had precedence over other boats. The packet boats belonging to the Duke of Bridgewater carried curved blades on the prow, allegedly to cut the towlines of any boats that refused to get out of the way, although it is now thought that they may simply have been decorative or symbolic.

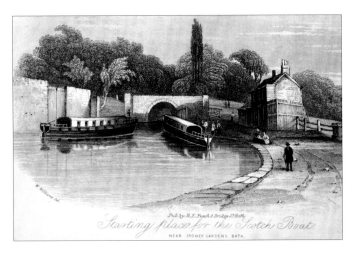

Despite the presence of a coal wharf here, a public swimming pool was built on the far side of the canal in 1869. This followed an Act of Parliament in 1867 to 'encourage the establishment of Public Bath and Wash Houses'. It was screened from view by corrugated iron, and was open to all men and boys above the age of eight 'except those who are intoxicated or disorderly'. It remained open until 1901, by which time it had acquired the name 'mud hole' – perhaps due to the activity of the coal merchants next door.

The wharf-side cottage was the packet station and boatman's cottage, with stabling. It was also a receiving station for the Bath Humane Society – hence the sign on the wall. Five shillings (25p) does not seem very much as a reward, but what this sign proves is that vandalism is not a modern phenomenon.

Left: During the years of dereliction, an angler quietly fishes from the towpath as it passes through Sydney Gardens. Today he would be knocked over by cyclists and jostled by walkers.

The towpath now enters a short tunnel which takes us into the very different scenery of Sydney Gardens. The gardens were opened in 1795 as pleasure grounds, with all sorts of features such as a labyrinth, swings, a sham castle, a grotto, and a hermit's cottage. Many of the events in the gardens, such as firework displays, happened at night, and many features seem to have been purpose built to encourage the sort of clandestine meetings that Georgette Heyer describes in her Regency novels set in Bath. When the K&ACC proposed coming through the gardens, the proprietors demanded 2,000 guineas (£2,100) in compensation – an enormous sum when you consider that the original cost of building the entire canal from Newbury to Bath was estimated at £420,000. The proprietors also demanded that the bridges and the tunnel entrances be ornamental. There was never any intention for the gardens to be accessible from the canal. It was only in the 1990s that a gateway was put in the wall bordering the towpath.

Having had to pay the owners of the gardens to compensate them for the horror of having the K&A coming through the gardens, it must have been infuriating for the canal company to find it was being advertised as a new attraction. Visitors were invited to enjoy the reflections on the 'placid bosom' of the canal, crossed by bridges 'in the manner of the Chinese'. The bridges were made at Coalbrookdale, and supplied to the K&ACC by the Bath firm of Stotherts.

However, sometimes things can go horribly wrong with canals, and it was certainly not an asset to the gardens in 1898, when there was a substantial leak, as the *Bath & County Graphic* somewhat gleefully reported.

The gardens themselves went into decline after the railway came through in 1841. Despite this, it appears that maintenance work on canal property still had to be

Above: Two early views of the canal passing through Sydney Gardens.

Opposite page, top: A report from the *Bath & County Graphic* for August 1898.

Opposite page, bottom left: In this early twentieth century view, a workman has taken up a very precarious position to repair the bridge. The gazebo in the background was shorn of its wings by the council in the 1930s.

Opposite page, bottom right: The portal of the eastern tunnel, being examined by Biggles the Bichon Frise.

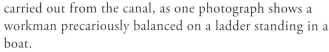

carried out from the canal, as one photograph shows a workman precariously balanced on a ladder standing in a boat.

Many features of the gardens were already in decay by this time. An elegant serpentine gazebo near the canal was ruthlessly mutilated and shorn of its wings, while the two little cherubs which stood guard over the central rotunda were removed – all in the name of restoration. Despite a protest from such an august expert as Sir Ambrose Heal, the wings were never rebuilt, and the stumpy remnant stands today as a monument to the philistinism of Bath City Council in the 1930s.

As requested by the proprietors, not only were the bridges ornamental – and specially designed by John Rennie – but the tunnel entrances had to be decorative as well. Originally, there were no railings along the towpath in the tunnel – these are a recent addition – but the protective covering on the arch is much earlier, as it bears rope-marks.

Above: The carvings above the portals of the tunnels in Sydney Gardens.

Below: Masons' marks on the tunnel walls.

Above the eastern portal is the carving of an old man; while the carving over the western portal is of a young woman. As the canal links the country's two most famous rivers, it is thought that these two faces represent Old Father Thames and Sabrina, Spirit of the Severn.

The stonework inside the tunnels is scored with strange geometric shapes. These are masons' marks, which have been studied by many experts, as they form a particularly fine collection. Some indicate which mason carried out a particular piece of work, while others may be approval marks, to show the work was done satisfactorily.

As you go through the western tunnel, look up in the roof to see where a block appear to be missing. The explanation for this – or a possible explanation – will become obvious when you are clear of the tunnel. Immediately on leaving the tunnel, the towpath changes sides on a particularly fine roving bridge. No untying of the towrope was necessary – the horse just walked up the ramp on this side, across the bridge and down the ramp on the other. To enable the rope to slide across easily, there are metal bars on the bridge.

Looking back, you will notice that there is a large building over the tunnel. This was Cleveland House, the headquarters of the K&ACC. We are so used to purpose-built office blocks that it does not occur to us that there is anything unusual about them, but there are very few which date from the Georgian period. The Customs House at Portsmouth is the earliest known example, but it is not as splendid as this. Inside, there is a grand staircase for the board members of the company and their friends, and a much more workaday staircase at the other end for the staff. The boardroom is twice the height of the other rooms.

For a long time it was said that the hole in the roof of the tunnel was to pass messages down to the crews of vessels. However, anyone who has been inside will know that this is impossible – the chute does not go directly down from the cellars to the tunnel – there is a bend in it. One theory put forward was that it was used for the disposal of ash from the building, but no self-respecting employee of a canal company would dump stuff into a canal. But here is my theory. Leaning over the entrance to the shaft inside the building, it is noticeable that the sounds from the tunnel are amplified. I therefore suspect that messages were passed to and fro via this shaft but that they were verbal messages – it was a kind of speaking trumpet.

In the early 1960s, one of the boats you might have seen trundling up and down the short section of canal that was navigable at this end was the *Charlotte Dundas*. She had side-mounted paddle-wheels and had been built by Lt-Cmdr Wray-Bliss, using a hulk found in the canal at Bathampton. Her function was twofold: to run passenger trips, but also – and more importantly – to chew up the weed which was clogging the canal. On one occasion, when, due to appalling weather, there were no passengers, Wray-Bliss insisted, to the dismay of his crew, on making the scheduled trip, as in his view weed-clearing was essential.

It had been a problem for years. In his account from 1928, CH Smith described the canal from here to the River Avon as being 'as full of weed as it could be; not only weed which grows off the bottom but also large lumps of floating blanket weed which, once it hits the propeller, you are finished'. It was this that the *Charlotte Dundas* was designed to combat. She was frequently seen on the section between Bath Top Lock and Bathampton, which was then regarded as the limit of navigation on the canal, although it is recorded that she once daringly made a journey as far as Claverton.

Sydney Wharf is on the opposite side of the canal from the towpath. The buildings there dated from the time of the canal's construction. In the K&A's heyday, the wharf was a busy place, with stables, blacksmiths, warehouses, builders' yards, and so on. George Stothert had a warehouse here. A fly-boat operator and canal carrier who rejoiced in the name of Euclid Shaw was established here as early as 1812. The Peacock family were associated with running the wharf for many years, so much so that part of it became known as Peacock's Wharf. By 1895, the warehouse was owned by a Mrs Tucker. However, as can be seen from the photograph

Cleveland House with its fine roving bridge in the 1890s.

Charlotte Dundas, the first of Lt-Cmdr Wray-Bliss's paddle-boats designed to chop up the invasive duck weed while offering boat trips, makes its way towards Sydney Wharf in the 1960s.

on the left, by then the rest of the buildings were ominously derelict, and there were no boats tied up.

By 1901, even Mrs Tucker had abandoned Sydney Wharf. However, many buildings remained, and some became comfortable little houses. Others, however, became shabby and some fell into ruin. Richardson's Carriage Works, on the corner of Sydney Wharf and Bathwick Hill, became a garage, with its shed-like workshops facing out across the canal.

By the mid 1980s, the clean-up of the area was gathering pace. Houses became spick and span as the area became fashionable, and narrowboats began mooring at the wharf once again.

At this point, the towpath climbs up steeply to the road, and the setts (not cobbles) are pitched – that is to say, they are set at a slight angle so that on icy or wet days, the horses would not slip. The handrail, like that at Semington Junction, is fish-belly rail from the Avon & Gloucestershire Railway.

Various trip boats have come and gone. The K&A Trust has trip boats at points along the canal and the one at Bath

is called *Jubilee*. Some Bathonians will recall that Lt-Cmdr Wray-Bliss later built a much larger version of the *Charlotte Dundas* called the *Jane Austen*. She was then replaced with the *John Rennie*, which used to moor up here at Sydney Wharf, behind Richardson's Garage.

Today, Sydney Wharf looks very different. It is home to Bath Narrowboats, which has a smart new office, from where boats, including day-boats, can be hired. They also operate the refurbished *John Rennie*, which can be hired for luxurious cruises to Bradford on Avon. The wharf is now overlooked by retirement homes called The Moorings.

As befits one of Bath's more elegant streets, Bathwick Hill was provided with a very smart bridge over the canal. The completion of the canal coincided with the development of Bathwick Hill. Before about 1810, it had been a rough track, bordered by a stream, and known simply as the road to Claverton. Unfortunately, access from the bridge is not wheelchair-friendly, as the way back on to the towpath, which once again changes sides

Left: Sydney Wharf in the 1980s, from the slope leading up to Bathwick Hill. The handrail is fish-belly rail from the Avon & Gloucestershire Railway, while the pitched setts on the slope prevented slipping on icy days like this.

Below left: The replacement for the *Jane Austen* was the *John Rennie*. It is seen here in the 1980s, moored up at Sydney Wharf behind what was then Richardson's Garage.

Below right: The same scene today, with the Moorings retirement flats and the Bath Narrowboats boatyard.

THE CANAL   BATH

Top left: A Victorian lantern slide of Bathwick Hill Bridge.

Bottom left: World War I soldiers messing about in a boat, with an admiring crowd of little – and one not so little – boys, with Bathwick Hill Bridge in the background. They might be in training or simply enjoying a day out while recuperating.

Top: More admiring little boys standing in almost the same spot – this time watching *Charlotte Dundas* on her way to Top Lock.

Above: Even in the 1960s, soldiers could be seen messing about in boats on this stretch of the canal. Today, exciting activities like this would be restricted by the number of moored boats. The building with the strange chimney is the former maltings, which still bears the name 'Hugh Baird: Maltsters' today. It is now a house and offices.

A view of the maltings around 1905, with barges belonging to the Hawkins Brothers, coal merchants and boat owners of 2 Sydney Wharf, moored up alongside the coal wharf.

The coal wharf, which was owned by the Somersetshire Coal Canal Company is seen here in the 1850s. The advertisement on the right dates from around the same time.

after you cross the road, is down a steep flight of steps. In the days of horse-drawn boats, the horse would come up the ramp, walk down the hill and on to Sydney Wharf, but today the way under the bridge is closed off unless you are going to Bath Narrowboats.

Immediately after the bridge was another wharf, again on the other side of the canal from the towpath. Many of the grand houses whose gardens run down to the canal were built after it opened, and there is a strange mixture of grand housing and industrial buildings. These include an old malthouse and a coal wharf – both now converted to housing and offices. During World War I, many soldiers were billeted in these old houses.

The next lock is at the top of the Widcombe flight. In 1976 a curious ceremony took place when the whole flight was officially opened, and

COAL, FREE FROM DUST.

NEWCASTLE, WALLS-END, & CANNEL COALS.

FREDERIC SPENCER,

SOMERSET COAL WHARF,

12, SYDNEY BUILDINGS, BATHWICK,

Begs the attention of the Nobility, Clergy, Gentry, and the Public at large, to the above Superior Coals, which have been procured from the best Pits, and can be confidently recommended.

F. S. has also constantly on Sale,

SOMERSET, FOREST OF DEAN, & ANTHRACITE COALS;

Also, a very Superior Coal for Bakers, and others, requiring strong and quick heat.

Orders received at the Somerset Coal Canal Office, No. 7, Char-lotte Street, Queen Square, and at the Wharf.

Above: Repairs under way at Top Lock in July 1973, with the terraces and crescents of Bath as a backdrop.

Left: The footbridge at Widcombe Top Lock.

Far left: An Edwardian view of Second Lock from Top Lock, showing the side pound.

Bottom left: During the air raids on Bath in April 1942, Second Lock suffered bomb damage.

Left: An early twentieth-century view across Second Lock towards Widcombe and Beechen Cliff.

Below: Abbey View Lock around 1910. The chimney is all that remains of the upper pumping station.

then locked up again until more of the canal was open. Still, as Peter Lindley Jones says, in his book about the restoration of the canal, it was a great incentive to the Bath branch of the K&A Trust.

A footbridge goes over the tail of Bath Top Lock, carrying a path which runs up the back of Bathwick Hill. The bridge, made by Stotherts, was loosely based on the Coalbrookdale ones supplied to the K&ACC for Sydney Gardens. Both this bridge and one further down the flight were afterthoughts, as they sit on top of the locks and are not built into them.

There is another lock-keeper's cottage at Top Lock – this time in the Gothick style. It is now a private house. The views from the Widcombe flight – if you are not too preoccupied with locks to take them in – are very fine. To the right are glimpses across the city, to the left are further views of Sydney Buildings, while straight ahead is Second Lock and the first of the side pounds which supply the flight with water. During the air raids on Bath in April 1942, Second Lock suffered bomb damage, and the windows of nearby houses were blown out.

The next lock is Abbey View Lock, although on an OS map of 1886 it is called Rasamar Lock. It is also referred to as Horseshoe Bridge Lock. Just before it is what looks like a column with an urn on top. It is actually a chimney, all that remains of the pumping station halfway up the Widcombe flight. This was necessary because not enough water came down the canal to supply the locks, despite the side pounds. Sadly, the chimney is now in poor condition. Plans are in hand, however, to restore some of the features on this stretch of the canal, including the chimney and the Stothert bridges.

Just beyond the lock is a bridge carrying Horseshoe Walk over the canal. After the bridge, which has more metal rails, the canal widens slightly before coming to Wash House Lock. No explanation of this curious name appears to exist.

Wash House Lock, like Top Lock, has a Stothert bridge across it. They were probably added because the only way to cross these locks when operating them was by walking on the gates. People still do this today, even though most locks now have walkways, but on wet or icy days it was a dangerous procedure, and there was at least one death when a child fell in.

At last the flight turns the final corner and heads for the river. Now there are just two locks left – although there used to be three. Widcombe Basin was once a hive of industry. At the time of writing, some workshops are still standing, though they are in such poor condition that they are due for demolition. However, the buildings that will replace them should echo their rooflines. Two buildings which stood next to them – Canal Bridge House and Catherine Cottage – were demolished in the 1950s. Among those who worked in this row were a carpenter, a corn merchant, a coach builder, a builder, a cooper, a wheelwright, a farrier and a blacksmith. In 1900 Alfred White, an engineer, moved into the row, and by 1934 a garage – later known as Widcombe Garages and Morning Star Garages – was established here.

Top: An early nineteenth-century picture of Abbey View Bridge, or Tyning Bridge as it was then known, with Abbey View House on the right.

Above: A similar view from around 1910, when the rural idyll had given way to housing and a gasholder on Pulteney Road.

Right: The bottom gate of Abbey View Lock being craned out during restoration of the Widcombe Flight in the 1970s.

Top left: The Stothert bridge at Wash House Lock in the 1940s. The buildings on the right were demolished in 2010 to make way for eco-homes.

Left: The Stothert bridge in 2009, awaiting restoration as part of the refurbishment of the Widcombe flight.

Top right: The coal yard at the bottom of Widcombe Hill, served by a wharf on the canal, is seen here in 1966. Widcombe Social Club now occupies the site.

Bottom left: In this 1920s view of Bridge Lock the coal wharf can be seen in the centre of the picture.

Bottom right: The same view today, largely obscured by trees. Most of the buildings on the right in the previous photograph were still there at time of writing, but had reached such a state of dereliction that permission had been granted to demolish and redevelop the site.

Left: Bridge Lock around 1900. In the 1970s this was replaced by Widcombe Deep Lock, which combined the drop of Bridge and Chapel Locks, after the latter was destroyed by the construction of Rossiter Road.

Bottom left: Looking up from Chapel Lock to Canal Bridge and Bridge Lock in the 1960s.

Above: Canal Bridge in March 1974.

Below: Just over a year later, in April 1975, the old bridge had gone and work on building its replacement was well advanced.

Left: Work on Widcombe Deep Lock is well advanced, as the demolition of Canal Bridge gets under way. The chapel schoolroom, built on the site of the Canal Tavern, is on the left.

Top right: Another view of Widcombe Deep Lock in March 1974, after Canal Bridge had gone.

Centre right: A flotilla of boats pass through Widcombe Deep Lock during the official reopening of the Widcombe Flight in June 1976.

Bottom left: Looking west from Canal Bridge over the ruins of Chapel Lock in March 1974.

Bottom right: Rossiter Road Bridge, built on the site of Chapel Lock, in February 1975.

Not everyone finds Widcombe Deep Lock easy to use. Here a Sally Boat has come to grief after the crew ignored signs to keep the boat clear of the cill.

On the far side of the basin there was a coal yard on Widcombe Wharf. In the 1850s it was run by Mrs Mary Merry, but it was later taken over by George Stockdon. Widcombe Social Club now occupies the site.

Lock 9, Bridge Lock, was once a perfectly normal lock. It is now Widcombe Deep Lock – three words which can strike terror into the novice boater's heart. It was necessary because a new road, called Rossiter Road, cut across the next lock – Lock 8 or Chapel Lock – which had to be removed. As a result, Bridge Lock had to be made as deep as the two locks together. The photographs on the preceding two pages give an idea of the scale of the undertaking.

The building of Widcombe Deep Lock has caused many problems – boats have got trapped in it, and work has had to be carried out on the house next door to stop it collapsing into it. If too many people use it before the water can be back-pumped to the top of the flight, the pound lowers alarmingly.

The bridge which carries Claverton Street today is a modern replacement. All that remains of the old bridge is the name of the four derelict buildings, whose address is Canal Bridge.

Chapel Lock was named after the Ebenezer Chapel, well known because of the words painted on its roof. Next door to it once stood the Canal Tavern, which the congregation finally managed to buy and demolish in order to build a schoolroom. This explains the inscription: 'Instead of the thorn shall come up the fir tree.' Clearly the pub had been a thorn in their side for a long time. West of the chapel was a row of houses called Waterloo Buildings. These too were demolished when Rossiter Road was built.

Finally we come the last lock before the river, Bottom Lock. Next to the lock is Thimble Mill. The mill may have existed for a considerable time before it was acquired by the K&ACC in the 1830s to use as a pumping station. Because many boats were only going part way up the flight, unloading or loading and then coming back, water was not being supplied properly. So the idea

Far left: Chapel and Bottom Locks around 1920. The chapel, with the writing on its roof, can be seen in the distance. Waterloo Buildings, on the right, were built shortly after the canal opened, their name celebrating Wellington's victory over Napoleon in 1815.

Left: The same view today. The chapel – and the writing – are still there but Rossiter Road now runs where Waterloo Buildings once stood.

Below: Looking east from Rossiter Road towards Bottom Lock in March 1985. A Travelodge now stands on the banks of the pound on the right.

Far left: Children line up for the photographer in this view of Bottom Lock from around 1906. Washing hangs on the line in the gardens of Waterloo Buildings. Chapel Lock and Canal Bridge can be seen in the distance.

Left: A photograph taken from the same spot a century later. Waterloo Buildings have gone, as have Chapel Lock and Canal Bridge, and Rossiter Road cuts through the centre of the picture. The canal, however, is busier than ever, albeit with pleasure rather than working boats, and the message on the chapel roof is still the same.

Below left: Anglers are still a common sight on the canal, but you are unlikely to find them huddled round Bottom Lock as they were when this photograph was taken in June 1971. Before the canal was restored, anglers had the canal pretty much to themselves, although whether they would find any water in it was another question.

Below: This view of the canal below Chapel Lock dates from the early days of restoration and contrasts vividly with the idyllic view of the pound on the previous page. Here volunteers are attempting to rescue fish as the water drains away.

was to pump extra water from the River Avon. Unfortunately, the mill owners downstream objected to this, and the company was told it could only pump from the bottom lock. Technology not being what it is today, the pumps were not up to this, so the company took to pumping from the lock with the bottom gates open. It did not take long for the mill owners to discover this subterfuge, and a stop was put to it. Today, modern back pumps generally keep the flight well supplied, except when someone has a disaster with Deep Lock.

Just beyond Bottom Lock is a bridge which carries a path towards Pulteney Bridge along Spring Gardens Road. For boaters, the choice is now between turning right and mooring up with a view of Parade Gardens and Bath Abbey, or turning left and heading downstream towards Bristol along the Avon Navigation – the subject of the next chapter.

We end this chapter on a celebratory note, with Sir John Knill, Chairman of Associated Canal Industries, and Kevin Gate, Director of the Bath Barge Company, standing by Pulteney Weir and raising a glass to the future of the K&A, after a new trip boat, the *Pride of Bath*, had been delivered in April 1983. Now refurbished and renamed the *Penny Lane*, this boat has taken many visitors and locals downstream on the Avon Navigation – the next part of our journey.

Top left: On 4 June 1976, the Widcombe Flight was officially reopened and then locked up again until April 1982, when it was possible to go all the way to Dundas Basin. Here the narrowboat carrying the official party, including the Mayor of Bath, leaves Bottom Lock on its way up the flight.

Top centre: The official party between Second Lock and Top Lock. The building on the right – a lock keeper's hut today – was the Bath Canal Centre, which sold books, leaflets and souvenirs to raise money and promote the work of the Trust

Top right: The official party arrives at Top Lock.

Above left: A flotilla of boats made the journey up the flight behind the official party. Here it is seen returning through Wash House Lock.

Above right: In April 1983, with the *Pride of Bath* moored up at Pulteney Weir, Sir John Knill and Kevin Gate drink to the future of the Kennet & Avon Canal.

7 Bath to Hanham: The Avon Navigation

For anyone embarking on this journey with a view to taking in all the various places of interest on the way, then Bath offers much for the visitor to discover. However, the city is not all Georgian elegance. The Museum of Bath at Work, in Julian Road, has exhibits proving that Bath had many other industries besides tourism. We will discover some of these in the next part of our journey.

From now on, we will be following – or attempting to follow – the Avon Navigation. From time to time, the path has to deviate. This is because, when the river was made navigable, boats – unless they used sails – were man-hauled. When the path changed sides, the hauling team just got on the boat and got off on the other side of the river. When a horse-towing path was finally added around 1812,

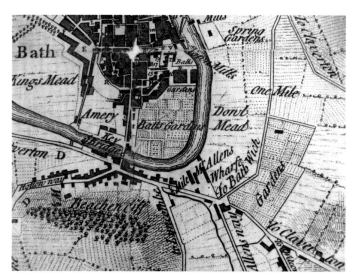

Above: An extract from Thomas Thorpe's Map of 1742.

Left: The White Hart Inn – now the Lock Keeper – beside the canal at Keynsham.

horse ferries rather than bridges were used to cross the river. Although these no longer operate, we are fortunate in being able to use the old Midland Railway line – now a cycle path – to cross the river.

If we look at an extract from Thomas Thorpe's 1742 Map of Bath, it shows Mr Allen's Wharf on the river, with a road called Mr Allen's Way heading south. This was Ralph Allen's tramway which brought stone from his quarries at Combe Down. The tramway crossed the road and continued to the wharf, where rough masons cut up the stone before it was loaded, by Mr Padmore's special crane, on to the waiting boats. JC Bourne's view of St James's Bridge (overleaf) appears to show that this wharf was still in use as late as 1841.

The Avon Navigation began slightly further upstream at Pulteney Weir, where there were mills. This was also where stone for building projects such as Queen Square was offloaded. Despite this, the main wharf area remained Broad Quay – or Key as Thomas Thorpe calls it.

The River Avon has always been prone to flooding. The great bend it makes around Bath slows down the water, and the Old Bridge, with its five arches, caused water to back up behind it. After a series of major floods in the 1960s, flood prevention measures were finally taken. Thomas Telford had been called in 140 years earlier to design flood defences after a disastrous flood in which lives were lost. However, the council jibbed at the cost of £48,000, and Telford walked out in disgust. His plans involved altering the profile of the river and replacing the Old Bridge with a single span – almost precisely the plan which was adopted in the 1960s.

Today, the river bank south of the station looks as though it has always been wooded, but in the mid 1960s, the slopes were bare, with just a few newly-planted trees.

Bottom left: Below Bottom Lock the canal joins the Avon Navigation. This was the view of the confluence around a century ago. Thimble Mill and Bottom Lock Bridge both survive, but all the buildings on the right have gone.

Right: The confluence of canal and river around 1970, with flood prevention work under way and newly-planted trees along the bank. Rossiter Road has yet to be built, and both Chapel Lock and Canal Bridge still stand, but Waterloo Buildings have already been demolished.

Above: In 1841, the GWR opened from London to Bristol and JC Bourne produced a series of engravings of the line. This is the view downstream through St James's Bridge, towards Widcombe and the junction with the canal. Allen's wharf was just beyond the bridge on the left, where goods can be seen piled up. The bridge caused immense problems during its construction, when it was nearly washed away in a flood. Flood prevention measures put in during the 1970s took away some of the bank, so that water now flows under the old pedestrian arch on the left, while the towpath is carried on a concrete platform.

Below: The view from Beechen Cliff in 2005. Trees now obscure the canal, although Thimble Mill – with the Travelodge behind it – can be made out on the right. The river now sweeps round in a smoother curve, allowing water to flow quickly under the single span bridges downstream.

The next part of the journey takes in a variety of bridges, each with a story to tell. The first bridge the towpath passes under is the Halfpenny Bridge. In 1842 a wooden toll bridge was built here, which cost a halfpenny to cross. In June 1877, when the Bath & West Show was held on Beechen Cliff, hundreds of people swarmed off an excursion train and on to the bridge. The toll-keeper was rather slow in taking the money and the bridge collapsed beneath the weight of the queue, with the loss of ten lives.

It was replaced with a metal bridge, which is still there today. The levels of floods between 1867 and 1960 are incised on the wall of the tower which holds the tollhouse.

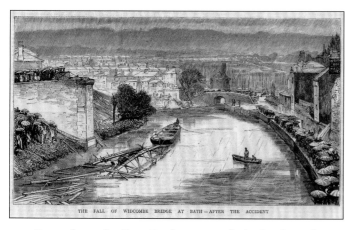

THE FALL OF WIDCOMBE BRIDGE AT BATH – AFTER THE ACCIDENT

Beyond it is the Skew Bridge, originally built of wood, which carries the railway over the river at such an oblique angle that, although the river is only 80 feet (24m) wide, the bridge is 164 feet (50m) long. Brunel used a form of laminated wood known as Kyanised, but it was replaced with a girder bridge after the Halfpenny Bridge disaster. Not everyone was in favour of the bridges Brunel built at Bath. In a *Guide to Bath* published in 1864, the Rev GN Wright declared that 'the railway bridges at Bath display great but unnecessary

ingenuity, and show how a simple and inexpensive object has been effected by means both complicated and costly.'

The path once led up to the Old Bridge – today you climb up to Churchill Footbridge. The Old Bridge justified its name, for it was one of the oldest structures in the city. There has been a bridge here since at least 1273, and possibly earlier. It was substantially rebuilt in the fifteenth century, with further changes over the years, especially in the eighteenth century, when it lost the little chapel which had given it the alternative name of St Lawrence's Bridge. During the 1840s and again in the 1870s, the bridge was widened to allow a broader carriageway and pedestrian walkways.

Finally, late in 1960, there was one flood too many and the Old Bridge was badly damaged. It was strengthened, and a bailey bridge was erected by the Wessex Regiment to take some of the load off it. Eventually, in 1964, after further floods, work began on demolishing it, and building not one but two replacements – Churchill Road Bridge and Churchill Footbridge. During the work, the bridge was dammed off, and archaeologists got a chance to look at the structure.

The Churchill Bridges were built with single arches spanning the river, to help speed the water away from the city. They were to be called the Southgate Bridges, but the death of Sir Winston Churchill in 1965 led to their current names being adopted. Even so, the floods have not entirely gone away. British Waterways insists on more headroom than this for bridges built now.

The towpath changes sides at this point, so cross the bridge and turn left. Leaving the Churchill Bridges behind, we walk along what is still known as Broad Quay, although there is little to show that boats once loaded and unloaded their cargoes here. Now, multi-storey blocks stand where once there were warehouses and maltings.

Top left: Bourne's picture of the Skew Bridge shows a horse-drawn boat heading upstream, probably towards the canal, and another, laden with what looks like blocks of stone, going under the bridge.

Top right: A similar view from about sixty years later. Brunel's bridge has been replaced with the girder bridge that is still there today, but otherwise little has changed. The house with a gable and a lot of windows, which can be seen in both pictures was the Cold Bath House, designed by the local architect Thomas Greenway in the early eighteenth century. Despite protests, it too was sacrificed to Rossiter Road. The mark of a gable on a building which has survived is the only reminder of it .

Bottom left: The Old Bridge in the mid-nineteenth century, with goods piled up on Broad Quay and Brunel's railway viaduct in the background.

Bottom right: A view of Broad Quay from the Old Bridge around 1905.

Above: The Old Bridge in the 1880s. The Full Moon Inn on the left was rebuilt in 1823, at the request of the K&ACC so that the towing path could continue on that side up to the junction with the canal. However, when the railway arrived the towpath was blocked for good. There was still a wharf on this side of the river, known as Kingston Wharf, however, as late as 1886. The large building in the distance, beside the Skew Bridge, was the original GWR goods shed, which was demolished in the 1890s.

Left: The Old Bridge during one of the major floods in the 1960s. Despite the waters raging inches below, Bathonians were still walking across the bridge looking quite unconcerned.

Top left: The Old Bridge with the Wessex Bailey Bridge in the background during the floods of November 1963. All the buildings lining Broad Quay on the right bank have since been demolished.

Above: A view from roughly the same spot showing Churchill road bridge, probably taken during the flash flood in July 1968.

Bottom left: The Old Bridge just before demolition in 1964.

Below: Seven hundred years of history reduced to rubble.

This end of town never really made it in the elegance stakes, despite the presence of Norfolk Crescent and Green Park Buildings – of which Jane Austen had forebodings. Her concerns about 'the damps' were justified, given the propensity for the river to flood, so this section of the towpath remained largely industrial. When the Midland Railway arrived in 1869, with a new station at Green Park and a large goods yard on the other side of the river, more industry was attracted to the area. Traffic also increased, so in 1905 a new bridge was built behind the western wing of Green Park Buildings. It was intended to take trams, but no lines were ever laid. It replaced a smaller bridge – which we will see later – thus opening up the bottom end of town.

The path passes the back of Sainsbury's, under a bridge that once carried Midland Railway trains but now provides road access to the supermarket and market stalls of Green Park. For a moment, Georgian elegance tries to step forward in the shape of Norfolk Buildings and Norfolk Crescent on one side, but Homebase car park on the other doesn't help.

The next bridge, Victoria Bridge, is the second of James Dredge's bridges on the canal. It was the prototype for all the others and, with its Egyptian-inspired towers, is the most impressive. Dredge later proposed rebuilding the Old Bridge to a similar design, but sadly the idea was never adopted.

The next bridge is the Destructor Bridge, so called because of the 'destructor' or waste incinerator that stood nearby. This bridge originally stood further upstream, near Green Park, and was moved here when the larger bridge – which we passed under earlier – was built.

After this comes an old railway bridge which carried a siding into the gasworks. Should the development of the Western Riverside ever go ahead, it is intended to demolish these two bridges and replace them with a new one.

The next bridge is the modern Windsor Bridge, which replaced the Twerton Suspension Bridge of 1837, believed to be one of the first cable-stay suspension bridges ever built. Then comes a disused Midland Railway bridge. After passing the Herman Miller factory, designed by two now

The new Midland Bridge being erected in 1905.

James Dredge's Victoria Bridge.

famous names in British architecture, Nicholas Grimshaw and Terry Farrell, we approach Weston Cut, or the Twerton Navigation, the longest cut on the Avon Navigation. According to the architect John Wood, he built it. However, this appears to be a typical Wood exaggeration, because the engineer was John Hore, who also built the Kennet Navigation.

Thorpe's Map of 1742, shows that, even by then, Twerton had many mills. They included cloth mills, paper mills and brass mills. Many of the brass workers came from the Low Countries, which explains why the island created by the cut became known as Dutch or Dutchman's Island.

There were several ferries along this stretch. The best known, just before the cut, was called the Royal Old Ferry. It lasted until April 1906, when it was replaced by a footbridge which is still there today. The ferry house and the buildings that dominated it have all gone.

In the early 1900s, the ferry appears to have been wound across the river by a chain and gearing system. In earlier times it was pulled across the river by a rope at shoulder height – a common method of working a ferry.

The cut was built to avoid two weirs, both shown on Thorpe's map. They still appear on an OS Map from the early 1900s, but only one remains. Today, there is a large bus depot on Dutchman's Island, reached by a new bridge across the river. However, following the towpath along the north side of the cut brings us to a bridge – known as Dolphin Bridge – with a stone bearing the date 1728. Despite its lopsided arch, it survived a near-direct hit during a bombing raid on the night of 26 April 1942. A nearby stable also survives, looking remarkably unchanged, as well as the Dolphin Inn, which was probably built at the same time as the cut. It suffered more seriously in the bombing, but was rebuilt and is now a thriving canalside pub.

Above: The steam dredger *Iron Duke*, built for the GWR by Stothert & Pitt to dredge the K&A. It was unpowered and had to be pulled or poled along, which may account for the number of men in the photograph. They are standing under the railway bridge that carried a siding into the gasworks. The Destructor Bridge can be seen in the background.

Below: An extract from Thomas Thorpe's Map of 1742, showing Twerton Navigation and mills. The Dolphin Inn can also be seen.

Ferry Twerton

Twerton Ferry shortly before it ceased operating in 1906. The building behind the ferryman's cottage was a tannery, with malthouses beyond it.

The Old Ferry, Twerton. Bath. 986.

The Old Ferry, Twerton. Bath. 995

Opposite page top: Looking down the main stream (on the left) and the cut (on the right). Dolphin Bridge is visible halfway down the cut.

Opposite page, bottom left: Here we see the ferry in the days when the area was still rural. However, on the north side, Bath was already spreading westwards. The ferryman seems to be a woman – not unusual, as we will see later.

Opposite page, bottom right: The ferry towards the end of its life.

Below: These mills at Twerton, built when confidence was high, have completely vanished.

Dolphin Bridge in the 1880s, with the Dolphin Inn on the right. Although badly damaged by bombing in 1942, the Dolphin was rebuilt, and, with its canalside garden, remains one of the most popular pubs to the west of Bath. Its name has nothing to do with sea creatures: in the eighteenth century, mooring posts on canal wharfs were known as dolphins.

A view back up the river around 1900, with Weston Lock at the entrance to the cut just in shot on the left. The metal rail on the wall in the foreground is still there. It allowed boats to be pulled smoothly into the lock against the current. If you look back up the river today, only the building with the gable end to the left of the pair of tall chimneys is still recognisable.

Weston Lock is not easy to negotiate even now for boats coming upstream, but the western end of the island has been made more user friendly since a new weir was built, lessening the cross-currents.

From here on, a hundred years ago, your route would have been distinctly rural, but industry has crept along both sides of the river. Manufacturing industries have gone, but offices have replaced them. Sadly, this industrialisation has meant that this stretch of the river is no longer considered suitable for a boathouse, and the site is now a scrapyard.

After passing under the old Midland Railway line again and crossing a bridge at the entrance to Newbridge Marina, you arrive at the New Bridge. Boaters will have a slightly better view of it, but the best place to see it from is the cycle path. And it is an impressive sight, approached by causeways raised above the flood plain, with side arches to allow the river, when in spate, to flow through.

The first New Bridge, built in the 1730s, was paid for by Ralph Allen. Like the present bridge, it had to have a high arch to allow boats to pass underneath. After a serious flood in 1741, it collapsed and a new New Bridge was built. This was the basis for the bridge that we see today. In the 1830s, it was repaired and widened – and evidence of the widening can still be seen as you walk underneath. You then have to climb up to the road, cross the bridge, and go down the ramp on the other side.

The path now follows the meandering River Avon. If the K&ACC had followed its original plan to build a canal from Bath to Bristol, rather than using the Avon Navigation, this section of the journey would undoubtedly have been much shorter. Walkers should watch out on the left for a brook coming under the GWR through a stone arch. Shortly after this, the towpath changed sides via a horse-ferry, but, as the ferry has long gone, you will have to remain on this side.

205. BOAT HOUSE—TWERTON.

Top: Where once there was once a boating station, there is now a scrapyard. Incredibly, this hut has survived, albeit in a very dilapidated state.

Above: The Midland Railway Bridge near New Bridge, shortly after it was replaced in 1934. The arches of New Bridge can just be made out in the background. Today, not only is the towpath a cycle path – the railway has been converted to a cycle path as well.

Opposite page top: A postcard view of New Bridge around 1910.

Opposite page centre: New Bridge after it was rebuilt for the first time.

Opposite page bottom: A view of New Bridge looking upstream in the 1890s. The ramp down to the towpath can be seen on the far side.

You soon arrive at Saltford, where there are boathouses and a new marina along the stretch known to rowers as Saltford Straight or the Long Reach. The first commercial boathouse here was Withey's, built in 1896. Clifton College already had its own boathouse here by then, however; this burnt down in 1894, and again in 1926. Sheppard's opened up in competition with Withey's in 1903. Eventually, they bought Withey's out, but had to do it secretly through a friend. Had the Withey family realised who the potential purchaser was, they would not have sold. The Riverside Inn is more or less on the site of Withey's Boathouse. Confusingly, the lock here is called Kelston Lock, as it is on the far side of the river and hence in Kelston Parish. We will meet Saltford Lock later.

The first recorded Saltford Regatta was in 1849. The course was a mile and a quarter long and began just above the lock. Regattas continued sporadically for the next few years, with temporary grandstands being erected, but by 1897 it was announced that the regatta 'may now be looked upon as an annual fixture'. It ceased during World War I, but the steam launches which had brought passengers to the regattas were used to give outings to recuperating servicemen.

Since there is no towpath on this side, the walker has to leave the riverbank and walk along the road known as The Shallows. On the right are brass mills. A group of Quakers began brass-making in the Bristol area around 1702. One of them, Abraham Darby, travelled to the Low Countries to bring back skilled workers, and there are many families with names of Dutch or German origin in Saltford, Ollis being perhaps the best known. In 1721, the company built a mill here and converted it to a Battery Mill, where brass ingots were worked into pans and dishes that were sent all over the world. Today it is cared for by a dedicated band of volunteers, and is sometimes open to the public.

Right: Clifton College Boathouse around 1910. Its replacement, built in 1926 in a similar style, still stands. It is now all part of Bristol University's boathouse complex.

Far right: Withey's Boathouse around 1904.

Below: Withey's Boathouse a decade later, after it had been smartened up. Withey's was a sizable operation, providing teas as well as hiring out boats. Sheppard's Boathouse, half hidden by trees, can be seen to the right. In the background is Saltford station.

Steam Launch, "Moss Rose" AT. Saltford. 42.5.

Top: This Edwardian postcard gives a closer view of Sheppard's Boathouse. Eventually Sheppard's took over the entire operation.

Above: A smartly dressed crowd watch one of the races at Saltford Regatta around 1910.

Top left: Kelston Lock around 1900. The lock-keeper's shelter has long gone.

Bottom left: The steam launch *Moss Rose* brings a party of recuperating soldiers out to Saltford during World War I. Some nurses can be seen aboard, also enjoying the outing. Kelston Lock is in the background.

Clockwise from top left:

Saltford Brass Mills from The Shallows. The mill was still operating when this photograph was taken around 1900. The gate in the foreground was the entrance to the footpath up to Saltford Station, which closed in 1970.

The Midland Railway crossed the river again at Saltford. Here maintenance work is being carried out on the bridge, with materials brought along the river by boat. The house with the timbered gable still stands.

A narrowboat approaching Saltford Lock around 1910.

Looking eastwards along Saltford Reach around 1910, with the boathouses in the distance. The ferryman lived in one of the cottages at the edge of the field.

Clockwise from above:
The ferry was operated by Hannah Gregory, who can be seen on this Edwardian postcard, with her home in the background.

Hannah Gregory with two passengers, perhaps coming from Kelston Station.

The Jolly Sailor and Saltford Lock seen from the other side of the river in 1982.

Kelston Brass Mills, across the river from the Jolly Sailor.

An aerial photograph of Saltford Lock in the 1920s.

The County Bridge. Keynsham.

Edwardian postcards of Saltford and Keynsham – clockwise from top left:

Looking downstream towards Saltford Lock.

Looking upstream towards Saltford Lock. The small building that can be seen in both views is still there.

A steam launch at Keynsham Lock, with County Bridge in the distance.

Another view of the entrance to Keynsham Lock.

A closer view of County Bridge, with Keynsham Brass Mills beyond it.

AVON BRIDGE   KEYNSHAM

One of the cottages which runs up the hillside at right angles to the road along the Shallows, just before the open space, was traditionally the home of the ferryman – or ferrywoman. After the Midland Railway was built, she would have been very busy, for a station opened across the river. Called 'Kelston for Saltford', it was one of the concessions forced from the railway company by the local landowner, Colonel Inigo Jones, for the privilege of taking the line across his land. Unfortunately, it was in the middle of a field and not convenient for either Kelston or Saltford. The only practicable way for Saltford people to reach it was to take the ferry.

The path returns to the river, where the Midland Railway crosses yet again. At this point, walkers have a choice. Those determined to stick to the river should climb up to the bridge, cross the river and go down the other side, following the path beside the river. This route also has the advantage of passing through the secret world of Kelston Brass Mills, with the workers' cottages, and a pleasant pub at Swineford, although those gasping with thirst will be glad to know there are also two on this side of the river. The disadvantage, however, is that you have to walk along a busy road for about half a mile. The official Avon Walkway takes another route, and this is the one we will follow. So continue under the bridge. If you need refreshment, one option is to turn left up the hill to reach the Bird in Hand, which was a pair of cottages until the navvies building the railway arrived, when it became a beerhouse. Continue along Mead Lane and go through the boatyard to reach the second pub – the Jolly Sailor – alongside Saltford Lock.

Boaters have to hug the left bank in order to approach the lock. The little lock-keeper's hut is still there. It was this lock which was blown up in 1738, in an attempt to stop coal being imported from Shropshire, in competition with coal mined locally in Somerset and Kingswood.

The Jolly Sailor was formerly a miller's house. The mill, which originally produced leather but was later converted to make paper, has gone. The house was certainly a pub by 1749, and possibly earlier. The fireplace in one room bears the marks of a curious initiation ceremony for mariners when they were appointed captain. A large nail was heated up in the fire and the novice captain had to pick it up in his bare hands and drill a hole in the fireplace.

From Saltford Lock, the Kelston Brass Mills can be seen on the other side of the river. From here, one should be able to follow the river, but the path is blocked by a garden – though quite what would happen if a horse-drawn boat came along is an interesting question – so walkers have to continue up Mead Lane, and turn right after passing part of the sewage works on the left. At last the towpath is reached, and following this will bring you to Swineford Lock, with a flock mill on the other side of the river. Swineford Flock Mill was a copper mill until the 1860s, when it was converted.

Once again the towpath changes sides, and once again walkers cannot follow. As late as 1900, the OS Map shows a horse ferry here. However, the Avon Walkway continues on this side until reaching another old railway bridge, which enables us to cross the river. This, though, is the last time the railway crosses the river.

On yet another meander, some works appear on the left bank, and then, as the river bends again, we arrive at Avon Wharf, the eastern terminus of the Avon & Gloucestershire Railway – more commonly known as the Dramway. This was owned by the K&ACC and carried coal down from the collieries of South Gloucestershire. We have already seen rails from the Dramway at Bath and Semington. Here we find stables, a weigh house, a workshop, and stone sleepers embedded in the ground around the wharf. The large house set in its own grounds was the headquarters of the railway.

Above left and centre: Bridges and tunnels on the Dramway, several of which survive, echoed the style of construction on the K&A. Here we see a bridge near Warmley and the portal of a tunnel south of Willsbridge.

Above right: The weigh house at Londonderry Wharf, the western terminus of the Dramway.

Left: The buildings at Avon Wharf, the eastern terminus of the Dramway, included stables, a workshop and another weigh house.

Below: Two views of Keynsham Brass Mills before production ceased in 1927.

Opposite page top: The view from Keynsham Lock in 1922, with the steel skeleton of Fry's factory at Somerdale being erected.

Opposite page centre: The same view with the factory complete.

Opposite page bottom: The factory in 2009, after Kraft announced its closure.

The river now heads towards another cut, at Keynsham. The building of this cut was opposed by the owner of the land, Henry Creswick. Despite coming from a notoriously litigious family, he was up against Ralph Allen and the Duke of Beaufort, so the sale of his land went ahead.

The bridge at Keynsham dated from the thirteenth century, and, because it marked the boundary between Somerset and Gloucestershire, was known as County Bridge. During the Monmouth Rebellion it was partly broken down by James II's men, but restored by Monmouth's. However, in the floods of July 1968, the bridge finally succumbed, and was washed away. It was replaced by a new bridge, and the river was diverted into a new course as part of flood prevention measures.

Before the river was diverted, it ran past more brass mills. These were the last working brass mills in the Bristol area, closing in June 1927. They now stand well back from the river, although part of the original meander was turned into a lake. They have been converted to the Brassmill Country Inn.

The brass mills, the bridge and the confluence of the Rivers Chew and Avon lie to our south as we head along the cut past the Lock Keeper Inn. This was originally a private house, where Monmouth's men are reputed to have slept after repairing County Bridge. It became an inn, called the White Hart, in 1719, and has also been known as the Ile D'Avon.

The photograph on page 126 shows it as it looked a century ago. Today, although the inn looks much the same, the scene has been transformed, with traffic diverted from the old canal bridge on to a new bridge to the west. Just past the new bridge is Keynsham Lock. Had you stood here in 1922, you would have seen construction work on a greenfield site ahead. This was Fry's Chocolate Factory, now, sadly, in the evening of its days. Fry's was taken over by Cadbury, who

did their best to obliterate Fry's name from the landscape, before announcing its closure. Kraft said they would rescue it – only to say, once they had bought out Cadbury, that it still had to close. For a community the size of Keynsham, this is a disaster. But, as we have seen, industries come and go – perhaps Keynsham will reinvent itself as Reading has done. But squeezed between Bath and Bristol, it will not be easy.

One industry that lasted for centuries but finally vanished from the area in 1963 was coal mining. However, the relics remain. We have already met one branch of the Dramway. Another branch came down to Londonderry Wharf, just over half a mile past Keynsham Lock. It was also known as Jack White's Corner, after a wharfinger who once lived here. There were gravel pits nearby, and a quarry with its own tramway which also ran down to the wharf.

A mile or so and another huge meander further on, our journey reaches its end at Hanham Mills. There is still a sense of remoteness here, even though there are two busy pubs. The Chequers was built as a private house about 1904, but the Old Lock and Weir (formerly and confusingly known as the Chequers Tavern) is about 300 years old. Its

website has an interesting local history page for those who want to know more. There is no longer a ferry, but at least two groups of oarsmen still row regularly up to the weir. The mill dates back to at least the seventeenth century.

Below Hanham Lock – Lock 1 on the K&A – the Port of Bristol Authority holds sway. Boats and walkers can continue to Bristol, but for those exploring the K&A, this is the end of our journey.

Opposite page top: Londonderry Wharf, or Jack White's Corner as it looked around 1910.

Opposite page bottom: Hanham Lock around 1910.

Above left: A woman waits with her son for the Hanham Mills ferry around 1905.

Above right: A few years later the scene had been transformed by the building of the Chequers Hotel.

Below: A working boat moored up opposite Hanham Lock – the end of the Avon Navigation – some time before World War I.

8 Downstream to Bristol

Although Hanham Mills is the end of the canal, the whole reason for its existence was to link London with Bristol. Boaters will almost certainly want to continue to Bristol, where there are moorings in the Floating Harbour. Walkers and cyclists can carry on as well, although they may find the route rather daunting in places between Hanham Mills and Bristol.

It starts off well, with the path continuing along the wooded banks of the Avon as it sweeps round in a great curve. At Conham, there is a ferry across to Beese's Tea Gardens. The ferry is said to be the oldest on the River Avon, and the rooms were founded in 1846 by Mrs Beese, the wife of the ferryman.

The river then meanders back to Crew's Hole. This area was industrialised as early as the eighteenth century, with the river used to ship goods out. In 1843, Brunel opened a tarworks here to make creosote for railway sleepers. It was run and later owned by an employee of his, William Butler, and only closed in 1981. Now there is a housing estate called Quayside Village.

From now on, housing and industry encroach increasingly. At Netham, the river continues over a weir, while boats bear right through Netham Lock and along the Feeder. This was built by William Jessop in 1809 as part of the improvements to Bristol Harbour. Liverpool was competing with Bristol for the tobacco trade, and the Floating Harbour was built so that boats could moor up in Bristol and stay afloat. The Feeder allowed them to continue upstream to Bath. It also alleviated the problem of water stagnation in the Floating Harbour.

Opposite: Heading downstream to Bristol from Hanham around 1900.

The River Avon Trail follows the meander, but, whichever route you take, it is all very industrialised. Although Bristol's docks long ago moved out to Avonmouth, the city is still full of industry. So the best course for boaters is to continue on down the Feeder, and at Totterdown Basin to go, via Bristol

Looking across to Beese's Tea Gardens and ferry in 1910 ... and 2010.

153

Clockwise from top left:
Netham Lock, the entrance to the Feeder.

The Avon allowed boats to come up into
the heart of Bristol. This nineteenth century
engraving shows it as a hive of activity, with
Bristol Bridge on the right, Welsh Back on the
left, and St Nicholas Church – dedicated to the
patron saint of sailors – in the centre.

Today many warehouses stand empty and
derelict, awaiting conversion into bijou
residences, and merchant vessels have been
replaced by motor cruisers.

The Granary – one of the most extravagant
examples of Bristol Byzantine architecture – was
built by William Venn Gough and Archibald
Ponton in 1869. In 1968 Acker Bilk opened a jazz
club there. It later became a rock venue but has
now been converted to apartments.

The main part of the docks in what is now called Bristol Centre was created out of the River Frome. Today, this is covered in, and traffic circulates where ships once moored.

Above: A paddle steamer negotiates the lock at the entrance to the floating harbour. around 1910. The lock dates from 1873 and has recently been the subject of a major restoration programme. The two earlier locks – by Jessop and Brunel – can be seen on the right, with bonded tobacco warehouses beyond them.

Below left: The schooner *Gypsy* lies broken on the notorious Horseshoe Bend in 1878.

Below right: Ships beached on the mud near Sea Mills in the early 1900s, waiting for the tide to float them off.

Opposite page: Clifton Suspension Bridge – iconic symbol of Bristol's engineering enterprise – seen from Rownham Ferry in the 1890s.

Bridge, to the Floating Harbour. Walkers may prefer to head for Temple Meads Station, where following the Brunel Mile will lead them by an interesting route to the dockside area.

The harbour was created out of the River Frome, which now flows under Bristol Centre into St Augustine's Reach. When Alexander Pope visited Bristol in 1732, he found, 'in the middle of the street, as far as you can see, hundreds of ships, their masts as thick as they can stand by one another, which is the oddest and most surprising thing imaginable'. Even well into the nineteenth century, the city centre was a forest of masts.

It would have been to these docks that Jim Hawkins and Long John Silver walked to find the *Hispaniola*, in Robert Louis Stevenson's *Treasure Island*. The Frome was covered over in the 1890s.

To accommodate the goods brought into the port and those waiting to go out, warehouses were built, in an increasingly extravagant style which became known as Bristol Byzantine. This culminated in the Granary on Welsh Back, now converted to housing and shops. Many others have also been converted, or are awaiting redevelopment, and the only ships you are likely to see in the inner harbour are pleasure boats, passenger ferries, floating bars, and houseboats.

The problem for Bristol was that the River Avon was tidal, leaving boats stranded on the mud at low tide. The Floating Harbour gave extra space for vessels to moor up safely, but even with Brunel's improvements in the 1830s and 1840s, the docks proved difficult to negotiate for the bigger ships that were being built.

The bends of the Avon below Bristol presented other hazards. Most notorious was Horseshoe Bend, which proved too much for some ships' captains. Sometimes they just ran aground, but the schooner *Gipsy*, belonging to the Waterford Steam Navigation Co, was not so lucky. Despite

being towed down the river by a tug, she struck rocks and mud in May 1878, before keeling over and blocking the river. It took five days to reopen the channel. The hulk was eventually dynamited some weeks later.

Despite the difficulties of the River Avon and its tidal fluctuations, and despite great damage suffered during World War II, the docks continued to operate until the 1960s. By then much trade had moved to Avonmouth.

Containerisation meant that cargo vessels being beached on the mud till the tide rose again was unacceptable.

Today, it is Avonmouth and the Royal Portbury Dock which are the modern face of Bristol's maritime heritage. Ironically, it was Brunel, with his desire to build ever larger ships, who initiated the decline of Bristol's docks, just as it was his GWR that led to the decline of the K&A. Yet for many, it is Brunel who symbolises the enterprise of Bristol, even though he was not a Bristolian. And it is with his Clifton Suspension Bridge, and its effortless leap across the Avon Gorge, that we end this journey.

9 The Somersetshire Coal Canal: A Brief History & A Short Walk

One of the reasons that the Kennet & Avon Canal prospered while others struggled was that feeding into it was the Somersetshire Coal Canal (SCC). In its heyday, this was possibly the most successful canal on the entire waterway system, paying a dividend of 7% in 1829, and an astonishing 8% in 1846. The trade, which then had to move on to the K&A, ensured dividends to the latter's shareholders which, if not in the SCC league, were comfortably pleasing – until the GWR took away the business.

It was the threat from Welsh coal which led to the canal being built. When the Monmouthshire Canal opened, Somersetshire colliery owners decided that they needed a canal as well. As John Rennie was already working for the newly formed K&ACC in the area, he was commissioned to make a survey and select the line of the canal. In 1794, the Act of Parliament was granted.

Building it was not without problems. To allow the Dunkerton arm of the canal to climb the hill at Combe Hay, it was decided to try out Robert Weldon's 'Patent Hydrostatick or Caisson Lock'. Recent research has shown that this was a sophisticated piece of equipment, but the geology was against it. The hills to the south of Bath include layers of fine clay called Fuller's Earth. This caused the chambers of the caisson to cave in, although not before several illustrious visitors, including the Prince of Wales and Jane Austen, had been to see it working. After a brief dalliance with an inclined plane, the proprietors reluctantly decided to build a flight of locks, known as the Bull's Nose due to a sharp bend halfway up.

This northern arm of the canal went past Dunkerton and Timsbury collieries, before ending, rather unspectacularly,

Opposite: The bottom of the Combe Hay Flight in April 2010.

at a basin in the middle of a field. The southern arm crossed the Midford Brook on an aqueduct west of Midford and was intended to carry on to Radstock. However, the failure of the caisson lock project and problems with water supply led to this arm of the canal being converted to a tramway.

The canal and tramway operated successfully for many years, until the arrival of the railways. The opening of a GWR line from Frome to Radstock heralded the end of the tramway from Midford to Radstock. In 1871 it was sold to the Somerset & Dorset Railway, which proceeded to build a line from Bath to Evercreech along much of its course. Ten years later, in 1881, the GWR opened a branch from Hallatrow to Camerton, robbing the canal of much of its remaining traffic.

In 1894 the SCC went into receivership. Having failed to find a buyer, it closed four years later. In 1903, however, a new colliery opened at Dunkerton. It was soon apparent that this was going to be the biggest pit in the Somerset Coalfield. The GWR, anxious to improve rail links to it, bought the canal and built a line along it, linking Dunkerton with the main line at Limpley Stoke.

The Camerton & Limpley Stoke Railway (C&LSR), as it was known, had a much shorter life than the canal. Dunkerton Colliery closed in 1925, but the line survived until 1951. It had one last moment of glory, however, when it was used in the filming of *The Titfield Thunderbolt*.

Parts of the coal canal are easily accessible, so here is a short walk along the canal. This is a virtual walk – another journey through time – and this book is not designed to go in your pocket. However, you do not need the book – just a map. Much of it follows the Limestone Link, and is clearly marked.

As we have seen in Chapter 6, the Coal Canal joined the K&A at Dundas Basin, where there was a regulating lock to prevent water flowing between the two canals. Canal companies jealously guarded their water supplies.

If the gate through the moorings is open, then walk beside the canal – otherwise take the lower path. If you can take the higher path, you will see that, although the canal is not being restored for navigation, this section is extremely busy. Yet even 25 years ago, this would have seemed

impossible. The bridge was filled in, and the lock converted to a rose garden. When Tim Wheeldon came to live in the lock-keeper's cottage, he had the vision to see that moorings were going to be needed when the K&A reopened. He dug out the lock, and acquired a bridge from the Oxford Canal.

The canal disappeared under the road, but this is now a dry dock. If you have walked up to the restaurant, you will be able to peer underneath, but not walk through. So, whichever route you took, you need to make your way to the car park and leave by the main exit. Turn right along the cycle path, following the trackbed of the C&LSR. Just beyond the brick bridge under the A36, the railway joined up with the canal. The playing field on your left is where, in *The Titfield Thunderbolt*, the cricket match was abandoned, with players and spectators rushing across the field to cheer the train as it whistled past.

Opposite page, top left: The entrance to the Somersetshire Coal Canal at Dundas Basin has been restored to provide a marina for boats travelling along the Kennet & Avon. A photograph of the junction of the two canals, taken when the Coal Canal was operational, and showing the regulating lock, is on page 94.

Opposite page, bottom left: The first few hundred yards of the Coal Canal, seen here in the early 1900s, with weed on the surface of the water, is now a busy marina. Dundas Aqueduct and the GWR main line along the Limpley Stoke valley can be seen in the distance.

Above: A view of the canal around 1890, looking east towards the bridge which took the canal under what is now the A36.

Opposite page, right: A photograph taken from virtually the same spot as the one above around 15 years later, showing how completely nature had reclaimed the canal.

Half a mile further on, you have to leave the canal and railway, and turn right up a footpath to the road. Turn left and left again down Mill Lane, past the old lock-up or blind house, until you reach a garage on your left, with two iron posts on either side – the remains of the level crossing gates.

Retrace your steps up the road, and turn left at the top. At the church, walk straight through the churchyard, out of the gate at the other end, and left down the road. As you drop down to Tucking Mill, you pass some houses on the left, with more houses on the right. Over to the right is the Somerset & Dorset Railway viaduct which is to form part of the Two Tunnels Path from Bath to Midford. The houses beside the road were once beside the canal and were part of a Fuller's Earth works. A tucking mill was a local name for a fulling mill. Some of the buildings, including one with a tall chimney, were demolished in the 1950s.

Just before the house on the right with Gothick windows, a path on the left takes you back to the canal. The house has a plaque stating that William Smith, the Father of Geology, lived there. In fact, the plaque is on the wrong house. Smith was employed by the Somersetshire Coal Canal Company (SCCC) as surveyor, and it was while working on the canal that he noticed the lines of different rocks which we know by the name he gave them – strata.

Following the path, you arrive at Midford. Before crossing the road, look back at the house now called Lowood. This was originally the weigh house for the SCC; its garden was the canal and the branch to the weigh house. A boat floated into the lock, the gates closed and the water drained out, leaving the boat suspended in a cradle, by which it could be weighed.

Gradually, Midford became a place of bridges. The road crosses the Midford Brook and the canal – the parapet is on your right as you emerge on to the road. Then the S&D built a viaduct and finally, when the C&LSR came, it too crossed further up the road before going through an arch

Above: The abandoned canal near Monkton Combe around 1900.

Opposite page top: Looking west along the canal at Monkton Combe in April 1890.

Opposite page, bottom left: The same view a decade later, with the canal falling into dereliction.

Opposite page, bottom right: Looking east along the canal from the other side of the bridge at Monkton Combe in the mid 1890s.

Above: Looking west along the canal around 1900. Tucking Mill is just out of sight around the corner. Midford Castle, a Gothick-style mansion dating from about 1775, can be seen on the hillside in the distance.

Below left: A drawing from around 1900 showing the Fuller's Earth works at Tucking Mill.

Below right: The canal being converted to a railway near Monkton Combe School in 1909.

Opposite page: The weigh house at Midford in 1890, with the bars of the cradle clearly visible, and weed already spreading over the tranquil surface of the canal. Midford Station was up on the left behind the wooden fence.

Midford around 1905 showing the weigh-house, with Midford Station behind it and the Somerset & Dorset viaduct on the left.

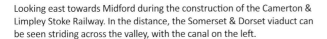

Looking east towards Midford during the construction of the Camerton & Limpley Stoke Railway. In the distance, the Somerset & Dorset viaduct can be seen striding across the valley, with the canal on the left.

The poor state of Midford Aqueduct before restoration.

Bob Honey (left), the landowner who allowed the restoration work to take place, despite problems such as the Foot and Mouth epidemic, toasts the successful completion of the project at the official opening in July 2002.

Midford Aqueduct today, with the new stone weathering to a more mellow colour.

Believed to be the earliest representation of a Somerset coalfield tramway wagon, this gravestone at Cameley records the death of 16-year-old Charles Sage at Timsbury on 17 December 1808. The *Bath Chronicle* reported that he was 'crushed between the post of a gate and a rail-road wagon and killed on the spot'.

of the S&D viaduct. This is where the opening shot of *The Titfield Thunderbolt* was filmed.

As the canal bridge is blocked, you will need to cross the road – this is a difficult crossing, so listen carefully as cars come round a blind corner. The path goes down beside a garden, under the viaduct and a road bridge taking Twinhoe Lane over the canal bed. Once over a stile, the canal opens up before you, hugging the contour line – unlike the C&LSR, which at this point headed across the valley to your left, on the other side of the Cam Brook.

On your left is the Midford Aqueduct, which took the southern arm of the canal over the Cam Brook. On the far side was Midford Basin, from where a tramway ran up to another canal basin at Twinhoe. The tramway was only intended to be temporary, but when the plan to link the two basins with caisson locks failed, it became permanent. From Twinhoe, the canal continued to Radstock. Problems with transhipment and water shortages, however, soon led to this section being abandoned, and the tramway extended along the towpath all the way to Radstock.

All that remains at Midford Basin, apart from humps and bumps in the ground, is a building known as the Powder House. It was thought to have been used for storing gunpowder although recent research makes this theory less likely.

The aqueduct itself is the grandest piece of architecture on the canal, and thanks to collaboration between various authorities, the Heritage Lottery Fund and the farmer, Mr Honey, it has been beautifully restored. The work had to be abandoned at one stage due to flooding, and Foot and Mouth restrictions also threatened the project. Many farmers might have given up at this stage – along the route of the canal various structures have been destroyed or damaged by farmers who have no interest in the canal or see it as a nuisance. Bob Honey is a shining example of a man who is prepared to be a good trustee of what he finds on his land. Despite the setbacks, he made arrangements with the construction team to ensure that work could continue and the restoration was finished at the end of 2001. Today, the new stone is mellowing down; in another decade, it is only the new date stone that will give the game away. Please note that the aqueduct itself is on private property and walkers should stay on the footpath.

Continuing along the towpath, there is an accommodation bridge which led up to what was once a pub, the Boatman's Arms. Shortly after this, a detour is necessary as the C&LSR passes overhead. Returning to the towpath, it should be noted that the path here was raised and used as a constructors' railway during the building of the C&LSR.

As you walk along, you will notice occasional locks – now very overgrown in places. You are gently beginning the ascent to Combe Hay – an ascent that will accelerate sharply at the point where the caissons should have been. First, you have to negotiate a kissing gate and a quick right and left to

Opposite page: The Camerton & Limpley Stoke viaduct east of Midford under construction in 1909. The rails laid by the contractor to supply the site ran along the towpath of the canal – by now looking very sad and sorry for itself.

Below: Locks on the bottom flight at Combe Hay in April 2010.

take you to the towpath on the other side. Look out here for remnants of the activities of another Fuller's Earth company, where fine clay was loaded on to the boats below.

At length the path leads you to a road, which you cross, passing under the C&LSR once again. You have reached the extraordinary flight of locks known as the Bull's Nose. One lock was lost when the railway was built, but the rest remain, in varying stages of decay, although members of the Somersetshire Coal Canal Society do their best – and it is a very good best – to keep them clear. The path follows up beside the flight.

Halfway up, the flight makes a sharp bend, almost doubling back on itself – it must have been most awkward to manoeuvre. The path does not follow the flight, but heads steeply up through the woods. At the top, you reach what appears to be another canal, but was a feeder for a pumping station, installed to give a good head of water. Remains of the pumping station can be seen. The path has been diverted away from the canal to give some peace and quiet to the residents of Caisson House, but the canal continued on, with extra locks at the top of the hill.

At the road, turn left, passing over the remains of the canal bridge. The canal was infilled here on the right, but Lock 1 is on the left. Turn right at the road junction to head into Combe Hay. Here you may wish to visit the Wheatsheaf, but enthusiasts will probably want to track down the aqueduct, which was converted to carry the railway. Turn right up the lane after the pub, and take a footpath on the left, leading down to a stream. (This should not be attempted if there is a lot of water in the stream.) The path drops ever closer to the stream until eventually you find yourself getting very intimate with the stream as it plunges under the embankment. That is your path. There is a raised way through the tunnel – there was always a path here, and the SCCC was forced to maintain it. As you go through – and you may well have to duck – watch out for the change in the tunnel roof, where the tunnel had to be widened to carry the railway.

To save going back through the tunnel (unless you really want to), continue on along the path. When it gets to the road, turn left down the track which will join up with Combe Hay Lane. Continue in the same direction until you reach the road junction. On your left is a wall built of engineering brick. This marks the eastern portal of Combe Hay Tunnel – a canal tunnel converted by the railway company for their trains.

To find the western portal, you must turn right down the lane to Dunkerton. Then you have several options. Going back to the junction and crossing down towards the main village is a pleasant walk. The Limestone Link, which you can rejoin by returning to Combe Hay Lane and walking downhill, continues on to Dunkerton, rejoining the canal just north of Carlingcott, and taking you all the way to Timsbury. There are many footpaths in the area, including, if you press on to Dunkerton, a chance to walk up the Fosse Way, which crossed the SCC on a rather charming hump-backed bridge, now demolished.

But our walk along the SCC ends here, having given you a flavour of the canal and shown you the two highlights – the Midford Aqueduct and the Bull's Nose.

Left: The top flight at Combe Hay in August 1932: (top) Lock No. 8; (centre) Lock No 9; (bottom) winding gear rusting away on one of the gates.

Far left: A sketch of the canal at Dunkerton from around 1900.

Opposite page: Combe Hay Tunnel in 1890. The house in the background is still there, as is the tunnel – deepened to accommodate trains on the Camerton & Limpley Stoke line – but any hope of producing a present-day version of this view is precluded by the vegetation that has now taken over the site.

10 The Wilts & Berks Canal: A Short Overview of a Long, Sad Story

If the Somersetshire Coal Canal was the prime example of a successful canal, then the Wilts & Berks (W&B) was the classic example of what can go wrong. The estimates of the cost were wrong, there were water shortages, but above all, it could not sustain enough trade. On the K&A, trade was two-way – goods travelled up and down the canal. The SCC was so short that it did not need a two-way trade – it was dedicated to shifting coal from busy collieries, and it was good at what it did. But the W&B wandered around all over Wiltshire and Berkshire, never quite getting to important centres as the K&A had done. Instead, there were branches off to places like Calne, Chippenham and Wantage. Competition closed off various options – the Oxford Canal Company, for example, refused to take coal that had come by the W&B, preferring to use suppliers from the Midlands. There were disputes with the K&ACC and with the SCCC.

In addition, the SCC could not supply enough coal for the coal-starved counties. The W&B needed another source, and it looked to the Forest of Dean. A link, called the North Wilts Canal, was built from Swindon to north of Cricklade, joining up with the Thames & Severn (T&S) Canal. This joined the Thames at Lechlade, giving another route to the Thames. The main outlet was at Abingdon, although an early plan had been to carry it over the Thames on an aqueduct and join up with the Aylesbury arm of the Grand Junction Canal.

Like all the canals proposed during the period of canal-mania, it began with high hopes. In January 1793, a meeting was called by the Earl of Peterborough, who owned land near Dauntsey. Many other landowners attended, keen to improve

the value of their land with the promise of easy access. At that time, the Western Canal, as the prototype K&A was known, was going to come via Chippenham and Melksham. When it was decided to reroute it round Trowbridge, the plans for the W&B had to be changed, and the route made longer. No one saw any reason to worry. There were going to be 'vast profits', as one prospectus claimed. The proprietors engaged the services of the Whitworths, father and son, who had worked for the great canal innovator, James Brindley. However, the Whitworths managed to get things badly wrong. In the end, it took 15 years to build – from 1795 to 1810.

As LJ Dalby makes clear in his book about the Wilts & Berks, there were never any profitable years. The best it could manage was 24 years of what Dalby called 'near prosperity'. Then, in 1841, the GWR decided to build its engineering works in Swindon. The fate of the W&B was sealed – but it took a long time to die. Ironically, this was partly because the GWR used it to transport coal to its works.

It was not until 1897 that the then owners applied for a warrant of abandonment. Incredibly, however, if it had taken 15 years to build, it took 17 to close. Too many interests wanted it kept open. Streams, for example, had been diverted to supply it with water, under promises to farmers that the canal could be used to water cattle. So they wanted it retained. Swindon was divided – the traders wanted to see the back of it, but, despite its stagnant state, the towpath had become a right of way and the councils of both New and Old Town wanted to retain it. The T&S and the K&A wanted it kept as well – every time a boat came down the North Wilts Canal or the W&B, they got a lockful of water. But finally, in 1914, the act of closure was passed.

Opposite page: Looking down the Pewsham Flight in January 2009.

Almost a century on, however, the lost remains of the canal are slowly coming back to life. The Wilts & Berks Amenity Group is now the Wilts & Berks Canal Trust (W&BCT). Plans are afoot to link the K&A – via the Wilts & Berks and North Wilts Canals – to the Thames & Severn, and a new junction has been dug at Abingdon. However, several sections of the revived W&B will be completely new. Many sections of the old canal now have houses, shops and businesses on them. Swindon's notorious Magic Roundabout sits firmly across its route. There is much to be done, but what has been achieved in the face of incredible odds has been astonishing.

So here are a few glimpses of the W&B.

Shortly after leaving the K&A at Semington Junction (a picture of which appears on page 81), there was a typical W&B footbridge. They were drawbridges, like those seen in Dutch paintings.

One bridge that was different was Gallows Bridge. When the canal was first built, Melksham was quite small, not encircled by housing estates as it is today. In those days, Gallows Bridge was out in the country. Its curious name is, according to local legend, a reminder that sheep stealers were hanged close by. The site today is surrounded by houses and is at the Ruskin Avenue end of Pembroke Road.

At the junction of Forest and Sandridge Roads, there is a short stretch of brick wall, which is the parapet of Lowbourne Bridge. In 1909, large posters were printed and put around the area, warning that part of the bridge was 'in a condition of dilapidation and that the passage over that part of it may be attended with DANGER'. Despite that, the parapet on the far side still survives, and shows some of the patching, using iron bars.

From Melksham, the canal headed north-east, passing Lacock and Reybridge, where its existence is indicated by

A typical W&B footbridge. As the caption on this Edwardian postcard describes it as being near Melksham, it may be the first bridge after Semington Junction.

Gallows Bridge in 1905 – perhaps the most photographed feature on the W&B.

The parapet of Lowbourne Bridge still survives today.

The canal near Lowbourne Bridge on the north side of Melksham around 1905.

A bridge takes the footpath over the top lock at Pewsham.

names such as The Wharf. It is now possible to pick up the towpath at Reybridge and walk as far as Pewsham, where the Chippenham branch headed west. Much work has been carried out here to retrieve the locks from the undergrowth which covered them as recently as ten years ago.

A few miles further on, after the Stanley Aqueduct – whose collapse in 1901 finally spelt the demise of the canal – a branch turned off to the east to reach Calne via the River Marden. This was at a higher level, so locks were installed to take the canal up to it. These are being restored by the W&BCT. The route of the Calne branch can be followed through Castlefields Park. The canal is in water from Chaveywell Bridge almost as far as Bowood, and there are occasional boat trips.

Drawn by W.Westall A.R.A.   Engraved by E.Francis.

CALNE, FROM THE CANAL.

Above: Coate Reservoir, built to improve the supply of water on the W&B, seen here around 1900. Today this is Swindon's most popular leisure area.

Opposite page, clockwise from top left:
On the Calne branch, the River Marden was canalised, and a wharf created in the centre of town. This postcard shows it in the early twentieth century.

Chaveywell Bridge about 1999. Since then, much work has been done to rid the canal of weed.

Ken White's mural in Medgbury Road in the late 1990s. Despite having been repainted in 1983, it had once again faded. In 2009, Ken White repainted it again and it now glows with colour.

A W&B milestone stands incongruously in the middle of Swindon's Canal Walk ...

... but The Parade gives no clue that a canal once ran through it.

Town Lock at Calne in the early years of the nineteenth century.

Above: The Wantage branch, near the junction with the main canal, around 1910.

Opposite page, top: Another bridge, closer to Wantage, which is visible in the background. This photograph was taken in the early 1900s. Today, this area is surrounded by housing and industrial units.

Opposite page, bottom: The canal basin at Wantage, choked with weed, around 1905.

The main canal, meanwhile, continues its meandering course through Wiltshire, still succeeding in missing anywhere of any importance – although it gets perilously close to Wootton Bassett, where a substantial section is now in water. Eventually it reaches Swindon. South of Swindon, a pleasant section can be picked up and followed into town. You might wonder why, when the canal company so obstinately avoided anywhere of any size, it made an exception of Swindon. In fact, it didn't. Swindon in the early nineteenth century was confined to the Old Town, south of the canal. It only started to grow after the GWR arrived. Today, the route of the canal passes through a pedestrianised shopping centre. In Canal Walk, you will still find a milestone telling you that Semington is 26 miles away, but The Parade shows no sign of its watery origin.

On the way out of town, Fleming Way, built over the old canal, takes you past the end of Medgbury Road. On the end of one house is a mural showing the Golden Lion Bridge. It was the first mural ever created by local artist Ken White as part of a job creation scheme, teaching young people to paint. He painted it in 1976,

and it made his name. He went on to design the Virgin logo for Richard Branson. Repainted in 1983, the mural again faded, and, although this gave it a faintly period and dreamy quality, it looked a little shabby. So in 2009, Ken White repainted it yet again, at the request of the council. It now glows with colour.

One surviving relic of the canal is Coate Water. Built as a reservoir to provide a better head of water for the canal, Swindon acquired it, along with the canal, when it was abandoned. It was converted to a pleasure lake, and was recently voted Swindon's favourite place.

At Swindon, the North Wilts Canal headed north to Cricklade, while the W&B ambled off towards Berkshire. Its avoidance of Wantage seems almost perverse. It skirted it to the north, with a branch heading south to a basin in the town centre.

Opposite page: The junction of the Thames & Severn Canal and the River Thames at Inglesham, with the lock-keeper's roundhouse on the left. The lock at the entrance to the canal lies straight ahead.

Below: The Thames at Abingdon. The elegant iron bridge crosses over the mouth of the River Ock. The junction with the Wilts & Berks Canal is just out of shot, but part of the canal wharf is visible, looking overgrown and unused.

Bottom: St John's Lock at Lechlade, built to ensure sufficient water supply upstream to make this part of the Thames navigable.

Eventually, the canal reached the Thames at Abingdon, the junction coming in almost next to the mouth of the River Ock. In order to allow the towing path to cope with this, the company had to build an elegant iron bridge over the river mouth. It is still there today, and is often confused with the canal, as it bears the words 'Erected by the Wilts & Berks Canal Company'.

The North Wilts branch joined the T&S at Latton, north of Cricklade. Heading east, the T&S then joined the Thames at Inglesham, where the lock-keeper had one of the company's characteristic roundhouses with an inverted conical roof to collect rainwater.

The final work associated with the T&S, though not on it, is at Lechlade, where an extra lock, St John's Lock, was built to ensure that there was enough water upstream to keep this stretch of the Thames navigable.

11 Meeting People: Past and Present

One of the pleasures of a journey is the people you meet along the way. In this journey we have met many people – this chapter contains a gallery of pictures, covering 200 years of life along the K&A and featuring some of those who did not make it into earlier chapters.

Right: Firstly, we must not forget John Rennie, whose skill in creating the canal ensured its survival into modern times. We saw his portrait on page 4. Here is something more personal – an extract from a letter with his signature at the bottom.

The people you are most likely to meet when walking the canal are anglers. It's probable that as soon as the canal had fish in it, there were people angling. Over the years, anglers seem to have become more cheerful and ready to talk. It was not always so. When the K&A was just reawakening, the anglers had had it to themselves for years, and walkers and boaters came as something of a culture shock. Here are some fishermen at different times and places:

Opposite page: Two boys fishing by Harbutt's Mill at Bathampton in the early 1900s.

Right: In 1982, a young man enjoying a day's fishing near Pewsey caught something he did not expect. At the same time that he caught a fish, a pike caught it too – and wouldn't let go. Despite having too light a rod and line for the job, he skilfully played the pike until he was able to land it. Fortunately, I was on hand to capture the moment. This young man would now be in his mid forties. Is he still angling?

Far right: Two cheerful anglers near Fobney discuss the trials and tribulations of the day – their concerns about the canal, the pest of lads motor-cycling up and down the towpath, the pleasures of angling, and the prospect of having their picture in a book about the K&A. If they're reading this, I hope they are pleased I kept my promise to include them

Bottom right: At Bruce Tunnel and Dundas Aqueduct, there are large inscriptions commemorating two of the great and good – the Marquis of Ailesbury and Charles Dundas. But at Devizes, on Prison Bridge, there is a marble plaque to the memory of one of the canal's most faithful servants, John Blackwell, who was its engineer and superintended the work 'with fidelity, vigilance, and ability'.

Bottom far right: Underneath New Bridge, west of Bath, a workman left his own memorial. Carved deeply into the stone is the name R Corp. The surname Corp is rarely found outside Somerset. Given the sophisticated style of carving, it seems likely he was a stonemason.

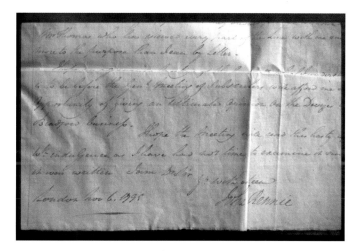

Here are some more stonemasons, this time from 1865, in a yard at Bath, next to what is now Widcombe Deep Lock. The company was owned by Samuel Rogers, who started in business around 1819 in the Carriage Road, later moving to 7 Claverton Buildings. By 1854 this yard was opened, presumably by Samuel Rogers Jr, who specialised in tombstones and monumental work. He retired in 1881, when Edward Rogers succeeded him. Samuel Rogers Jr may be the second from the right with the bowler hat.

Canals are ideal for shipping stone around, which may explain why there were so many stone yards near the K&A. Here are more masons, this time in the early 1930s, in the builder's yard of Axford & Smith Ltd. It was located next to the canal just off Pulteney Road in Bath, opposite Regent Terrace.

Top left: As we have already seen, during World War I the canal was use for training troops. Here a boatman looks on critically, while a notice advertising pleasure boats recalls happier times.

Bottom left: Soldiers take a break from exercises to pose for the photographer. How many of these young men made it back from the front?

Top right: At the forefront in maintaining the impetus to get the canal open was the Kennet & Avon Canal Trust. Running trip boats was a good way of raising awareness. The Trust boat at Bath today is the *Jubilee*. Before her came the *Dragonfly*, seen here being tried out for the first time in April 1984.

Bottom right: Children as well as adults helped to restore the canal after decades of neglect. Here a junior working party is seen on Caen Hill Flight in September 1974.

There were many events to raise money to restore the canal, and if people could enjoy themselves – so much the better! On 21 September 1974, the top four locks on the Widcombe Flight in Bath were opened, following their restoration by the Trust with grants from Bath City Council. The *Jane Austen* performed the official 'locking-up ceremony' before heading to Bathampton for a dinner dance, but, as this gallery of photos shows, Widcombe also took the opportunity to organise a carnival.

Opposite page, clockwise from top left: The Fayre on the towpath seen from Bathwick Hill Bridge; Sea Cadets rowing through Bathampton; Gordon Robins providing a musical accompaniment; the *Jane Austen* on its way up the flight

This page, clockwise from top left: The *Fistral* powers along the canal; one way of raising money was by taking a ducking in the canal; another of the craft taking part in the festivities; the Bath Arts Workshop helped organise the carnival – here Ralph Oswick (aka Lady Margaret) holds a lone vigil for unreason. Twenty-six years later, in 2010, Ralph – now artistic director of the Natural Theatre Company – organised another carnival – Widcombe Rising – to celebrate the canal's 200th anniversary.

Clockwise from top left: We should not forget all those professionals who have worked to get the canal back into shape. Here is part of the team putting in the concrete bed along the Limpley Stoke Valley.

Then there are the British Waterways staff, who have to fix things when sluices collapse (as here) or paddles break, or someone manages to empty the pound above Widcombe Deep Lock. We often dread the orange tape which means we have to leave the towpath for a stretch, or that a lock is temporarily closed – but without these people, the canal would soon grind to a halt.

British Waterways also maintains a presence at events such as the K&A 200 celebrations in Sydney Gardens.

Some have chosen to make a quiet living on the canal. This gentleman sells ice-cream and cheese, working his way along canals as he does so. It won't make him a fortune, but on a sunny September walkers were pleased to see him, and he was equally happy to chat.

Many people now live along the canal in boats of all kinds. The owner of this boat – which has no engine – has a minimal carbon footprint. So, in an age when climate change is a serious issue, perhaps we should be applauding him. But British Waterways wants him off the canal, not because he has not got a licence – he has – but because he does not obey the rule of moving the boat a certain distance every two weeks. It's just one example of how the different uses to which people want to put the canal may not be readily compatible.

Clockwise from top left: We should not forget the photographers who took the pictures in this book. A century ago, they did not have the option of using today's lightweight cameras. To get their shots, they had to cart masses of equipment around, often in wooden boxes. In this photograph, taken at Widcombe, the cameraman had to struggle with winter temperatures and then round up some little girls, wrapped up warmly in their winter coats, to pose against the balance beam.

To take an informal picture like this today is simple. A century ago, the photographer had to carry all his heavy equipment into Sydney Gardens tunnel before setting it up on the narrow towpath. If he dropped anything, it would have gone straight into the canal. His model had to pose in just the right place, and he had to gauge light and shade, aperture and shutter speed to come up with this beautifully composed shot, in which the lady takes your eye through the arch to the world beyond.

Today's digital cameras allow us to take shots that would have been very difficult a century ago. Here, James Fagan, a keen photographer as well as folk musician, gives us a chilly reminder that winter can bring canals as well as roads and rail to a standstill ...

... while here he gives us a boater's view of Widcombe Deep Lock.

12 Into the future: From Sleeping Princess to Queen of Waters

The Kennet & Avon Canal has been called the sleeping princess of the canal network. No longer is this true. It is busy with hire boats, private narrowboats, and people living on the canal. Walkers and cyclists use towpaths where once I strolled along a narrow path and saw no one. The great flight of locks at Devizes, whose dereliction moved me almost to tears is now back in use. But is the future secure?

People who make predictions in books often end up looking rather foolish. The future has surprises for us all. When we speak of tomorrow, the gods laugh, says the Chinese proverb. So all I intend to do in this chapter is to make some comments about issues that must be faced and where we – those of us who love the K&A – might go from here.

When the canal was completed in 1810, there were no celebrations. It had taken so long and cost so much. It was a different story in 1990, when it reopened. Then there was great enthusiasm and celebrations. The future certainly looked secure. However, it was not a future that everyone had anticipated for the canal. The co-founders of the Inland Waterways Association, Tom Rolt and Robert Aickman, fell out over what should be the future goal. Rolt had a romantic idea that the canals should continue as before, left to working boats but in the old-fashioned way. Aickman believed that there needed to be a commercial reason to justify their future, and proposed mixing working boats and leisure boats.

In the event neither aim has come to fruition. The canals, especially the K&A, are now mainly given over to pleasure boats, but decorated in a way Tom Rolt would have approved of. However, Aickman's dream of using the canals for commercial transport appears to have died. When he put his ideas forward, fuel was cheap, labour expensive, and the road lobby had the ascendency – this was in the days when motorway building was met with cheers not jeers, and when Dr Beeching was emasculating the rail system. Despite waterborne transport being eleven times more efficient than road travel, Aickman was seen as talking nonsense.

Today, we see things differently. Fuel costs have risen, new technologies mean solar-powered batteries and electric-powered engines are far more efficient. Carbon footprints are a matter of concern. All this makes waterborne transport look much more attractive. As I write this, a scheme to

Opposite page: A night-time scene in Bath, with a narrowboat moored up at the head of the Avon Navigation.

Right: A traditional canal scene recreated at the wharf in Bradford on Avon in September 1996 ... but the men and women who lived and worked on the canal on the nineteenth century would struggle to recognise the leisure-themed waterway of today.

use boats to transfer waste downstream from the council tip in Bath is being seriously considered. It is possible that Aickman may now be seen as the visionary he undoubtedly was.

In celebration of the 200th anniversary, it is good news that British Waterways is applying to upgrade the K&A to a cruiseway. Mark Stephens, its waterway manager, points out that

> British Waterways has, in reality, been managing the Kennet & Avon Canal as if it has had cruiseway status since its multi-million pound restoration. We think that the formalisation of this status is beneficial to the canal, helping to secure its long term future by legally stating that the canal should be maintained to a level whereby cruising craft, such as narrowboats, can safely navigate the length of the canal. Here at British Waterways we believe that this is the appropriate classification for this popular and much-loved waterway, which this year is celebrating its 200th anniversary ... The reclassification of the waterway during this the canal's bicentenary year would be especially poignant, and a way to acknowledge the amazing works undertaken by volunteers and partnership groups to save the canal from oblivion and turn it back into a thriving leisure resource, a piece of working heritage and a linear wildlife habitat. The Kennet & Avon Canal is regarded as a blueprint for successful waterway restoration and regeneration and the restored canal managed by British Waterways, working with volunteers from the local community and local authorities, is one of the inspirations behind plans to establish a new 'national trust' for the waterways.

More recently, it has been announced that British Waterways is one of the quangos to be dropped by the coalition government. Although this caused alarm, in fact it is good news. British Waterways has been looking at charitable status for some time now. This would release it from DEFRA, which has persistently underfunded it. It would be free to seek funding elsewhere, and to work more readily with volunteers, freed from government control.

That there are difficulties is obvious, not least in trying to reconcile the needs of all the different users. Walkers sometimes conflict with cyclists, and boaters with anglers. Then there is the issue of people living on the canal. However, cruiseway status would encourage more working boats. People seeking a slower pace of life are using narrowboats to trade. There is the Raft Café boat at Bathampton, the cheese boat we met at Dundas Basin, and one couple are using their boat as a floating wool shop.

All of this can only be good news. Climate change, recession, and unforeseen problems may lie ahead, but in the year we celebrate K&A 200, the future looks promising for the Queen of Waters.

Opposite page, left: The logo celebrating the 200th anniversary of the canal.

Opposite page, right: In the winter of 2009/2010, no one was going anywhere on the canal, as the ice closed in. However, it was nothing like as severe as the great freeze of 1962/1963, when even the River Avon froze. With climate change, hard winters like this become less frequent, and ice-breakers are now a rare sight on southern canals.

Below: A toast to the future of the Kennet & Avon – Queen of Waters.

Appendix 1: Some FAQs about Canals

What is a canal and how does it differ from a river navigation?

A canal is a man-made waterway. Canals come in many sizes, from great ship canals like the Suez and Panama Canals down to tub boat canals on which goods were carried in unmanned little tubs floated or hauled downstream.

A river navigation is created when a river is made navigable by introducing locks and cuts. Rivers often became unnavigable when weirs were built across them to ensure a water-supply for watermills. Rivers can also be very winding. Hence some canalised sections are short, with locks to avoid weirs – others are much longer to avoid a series of bends in the river, and almost amount to short canals in their own right.

Confusingly, canals are also known as navigations. The men who built them were known as navigators – later shortened to navvies.

What are locks for, and how do they work?

Basically, locks allow boats to travel up or down hill. The simplest locks were called flash or staunch locks – none survive on the K&A, although Blake's Lock at Reading was once of this type. Staunch locks had just one gate and acted as a dam. If you were on the downstream side going upstream, and your boat started to run aground, you had to go to the last lock below your boat and close the gate, thus getting the river to rise. You then floated up to the staunch lock, above you, opened the gate and floated through. If you met a weir, your boat would be winched up through the lock, over the weir.

Opposite: At the bottom of the Caen Hill Flight, September 2009.

Things were more exciting going the other way. Here, to get downstream, you closed the gate on the lock you were nearing. The water then rose. When there was sufficient water above the gate, you flung the gate open and travelled smartly downstream on the 'flash' of water.

Pound locks were invented by the Chinese in the tenth century, but were not introduced into this country until 1563, when the Exeter Canal was built. They are ideal for canals as they do not rely on running water but on having a pound of water above them to provide the water supply. (A pound is simply the stretch of water between two locks – the word has the same root as pond.)

Pound locks have two sets of gates, each equipped with sluices known as paddles. Those on the top gate are usually ground paddles, which means that when the paddles are raised, the water enters the lock via a sluice through the side of the lock rather than directly through the gate – thus avoiding the risk of the boat being flooded. On the lower gates, this risk does not exist, so the gate has the paddles.

When coming up through the lock, the gates are closed until the lock is emptied by opening the gate paddles. When it is empty, the paddles are lowered again, the boat sails in and the gates are closed. Then the ground paddles are opened, allowing water in from the upper pound, and the boat rises. When the lock is full, the top gates can be opened, and the boat sails off – after lowering the paddles again. The reverse procedure happens, going the other way.

The only drawback to this is that every time you use a lock, an entire lockful of water goes down to the next pound. On rivers, this doesn't matter, because normally there is more water coming down, but it means that canals have to have very good water supplies on summit levels. Every time a boat crosses a summit, two lockfuls of water go from the summit pound.

How does the water get into a canal, and why does it stay there?

Water gets into canals in a number of ways. Rain is the most obvious, though what is gained in rainfall is probably lost in subsequent evaporation. Streams and springs often drain into them, and culverts may be built to encourage this. One of the complaints that farmers made when the Wilts &Berks Canal was built was that they might lose the means of watering sheep and cattle.

Rivers may supply the water. Even though the K&A becomes more recognisably a man-made waterway after Newbury, it still takes water from the River Kennet. At the other end of the canal, it takes water from the River Avon, but here it has to be pumped up, as the river is below the level of the canal. The older pumps have now been replaced by much more efficient electric pumps, and this technology has also allowed water to be back-pumped up flights, such as Devizes and Widcombe, and at Bradford on Avon.

At the summit level, the main supply is from Wilton Water, and again the water has to be pumped up. The water then flows along a leat to the summit level itself.

Water stays in the canal because of the way it is built. Traditionally, canals were clay-puddled – that is, the bottom was lined with clay and since it was kept wet, it did not dry out and did not allow water out of it. However, animals burrowing into it were liable to create leaks, so lengthsmen had to check for the burrows of water rats. It also explains why you should not punt on a canal.

In the sections of the canal which pass along the Avon Valley, and which were prone to bursts caused by landslips, a new method has been tried out, using a waterproof lining covered in concrete. Some of the people who live on the canal are anxious about this, as they say it has made the canal rigid, and that as a train passes by on the nearby main line from Paddington, the canal shivers. However, it appears to be working at the moment. As the man who fell from the top of the Empire State Building was heard to say as he passed the 19th floor – so far, so good.

What is the difference between a barge and a narrowboat?

In essence, a barge is twice the width of a narrowboat. Canals are defined by the width of their locks. Narrow canals have narrow locks which will only take – you've guessed it – narrowboats. The advantage is that they use less water. Wide canals, like the K&A , have double-width locks, which will take one barge, or two narrowboats abreast. Despite problems with water supplies, the canal had to be like that, as it needed to take Newbury barges. Today, this means that you will often see Dutch barges moored along it. However, some boats were not as wide as barges but wider than narrowboats – they were therefore known as wide boats. On the K&A they were also known as mules.

Purists insist there is a difference between narrow boats (two words) and narrowboats (one word). The former, they say, are the original working boats designed for transporting goods throughout the canal network, while the latter are modern craft designed for leisure. Since what you see today on canals may be a complete mixture of old boats converted, new builds and working boats, I have refused to get tangled up in this controversy and referred to them all as narrowboats. But never call a narrowboat a barge or a longboat – the owners will be mortified.

Appendix 2: Mileages

Unless otherwise stated, the named points are served by rail

Town	Miles from Reading	Miles from Previous Stop	Notes
Reading	0	0	All services. Marina/boatyard on River Thames.
Theale	7	7	About 1 mile from canal. Station closer. Shops etc.
Aldermaston	10.75	3.75	K&A Trust tea room and souvenir shop. Marina/boatyard.
Woolhampton	12.85	2.1	Station is called Midgham – several pubs and shops in village.
Newbury	19.5	6.65	Pubs, shops, and K&A Trust building. Marinas/boatyards.
Kintbury	25	5.5	Pub by canal.
Hungerford	28	3	Pubs, shops, all very convenient for canal.
Froxfield	30.25	2.25	Short walk from canal – no station. Shops and pub.
Little Bedwyn	31.75	1.5	No station – noted for its top restaurant/pub, the Harrow.
Great Bedwyn	32.85	1.1	Station is called Bedwyn – pubs, shops.
Crofton	34.5	1.65	No Station. Pumping Station (if open) has shop and café.
Wootton Rivers	39	4.5	No station – pub.
Pewsey	41.75	2.75	Mile downhill into town Not quite as far to station. Two pubs by canal.
Honeystreet	45.75	4	No Station. Shops and pub.
Horton	51	5.25	No Station – Bridge Inn by canal.
Devizes	54	3	All facilities. No Station but good bus service.
Seend	58.5	4.5	No Station – Two pubs – Barge Inn on canal; Brewery Inn up hill.
Semington	60.5	2	No station. Shops etc in village. Somerset Arms pub.
Hilperton	63	2.5	Marina/boatyard. Station, shops and pubs in Trowbridge, 1 mile away.
Bradford on Avon	66.75	3.75	All facilities in town. Supermarket close to wharf. Marina/boatyard.
Avoncliff	67.25	0.5	Station is request stop. Cross Guns pub & tearooms.
Bathampton	73	5.75	No station. Bus from village or cross river to Batheaston. Pubs.
Bath (Widcombe)	75.25	2.25	All facilities. Widcombe has shops, pubs, and backpacker accommodation @ White Hart Inn.
Saltford	81	5.75	No Station. Pubs, shops. Marina/boatyard.
Keynsham	84.5	3.5	Station short walk up hill. All facilities in town. Pub near canal.
Hanham Mills.	86.5	2	No Station. Pubs.
Bristol Centre	92	5.5	All facilites.
Avonmouth	100	8	Bristol Docks. Served by Severn Beach line to Temple Meads.

Acknowledgements

First of all, I would like to thank my husband Dr. Andrew Swift for walking the whole length of the canal with me in September 2009, especially as he would prefer to be looking at railways. This explains why there are photographs of trains in a book about canals.

Special thanks are due to Nancy Fagan and James Kerr. I would firstly like to thank Nancy Kerr for allowing me to use the title of her song 'Queen of Waters', from the album *Twice Reflected Sun*, as the title of this book. I had only managed to think of the rather dull and frequently used 'Along the Kennet & Avon Canal', but after hearing her and James sing this at Trowbridge Village Pump Festival in 2010, I felt it was the title the book needed. To those who know and love the K&A in all its variety, it is indeed the Queen of Waters. James also contributed some photographs, and they took time from their busy schedule to write the foreword. Their friend Lizzy Doe, musician, artist and photographer, allowed me to use an image from her photoshoot of James and Nancy.

Gill Owen at British Waterways supplied me with up to date information about the bid to make the canal a cruiseway, and we had a helpful chat about the future of British Waterways. I am also grateful for permission to use the logo for K&A 200.

I owe a debt of thanks to all those who allowed me to use pictures from their collections. In selecting the images for this book, I avoided using the Kennet & Avon Canal Trust archive, as the pictures have been seen before in their own publications. I tracked down various sources besides our own collection to introduce to the public some pictures which I hope have not been widely seen before. These include some taken around 1890 showing the journey of Steam Launch *Eva*

along the K&A. Hitherto, these have only been published in *Archive* magazine as part of my article 'All about Eva'.

Many of the pictures come from our own collection, the Akeman Press Archive. Several of the colour pictures were taken by myself on my journeys along the canal, either on foot or on *NB Idlewild* in 1994. The modern colour pictures were mainly taken by Andrew or me. However, some were given us by the late Bruce Crofts, and some by Dennis Lanham and Geoffrey Hiscocks. Others come from my late mother's collection of slides – now all part of the Akeman Press Archive.

I was dismayed to be told that the eastern end of the canal, and the Kennet Navigation in particular, had not been widely photographed in the past. However, I have had some generous loans to allow me to augment the selection of pictures. The Local Studies Section of Reading Central Library allowed Andrew and I to photograph part of their collection, and the staff were unfailingly kind and helpful in sorting out the pictures for me. Gordon Collier loaned me some pictures of Wantage from his collection of postcards of the Wilts & Berks Canal. Hungerford Historical Association contributed some of their collection of images of Hungerford, such as the delightful picture of the cigarette race. This archive is known as the Hungerford Virtual Museum, and can be found on-line at *www. hungerfordvirtualmuseum.co.uk*.

At the western end of the canal, there was almost too much material to choose from – perhaps the fact that the canal went through Bath made it particularly attractive to photographers. In addition to our own collection, Paul De'Ath offered us a wonderful choice of fascinating postcards and photographs from his collection. Local photographer

Robert Coles also generously allowed us to use some of his photographs. Some Bath items come from Bath Central Library and Bath Record Office. Thanks are also due to Colin Johnston, archivist at Bath Record Office, for supplying me with copies of the 1886 OS map – an invaluable aid in following what has happened to the canal as it passes though Bath. Other pictures come from the *Bath Chronicle* Archive, and the present editor of the *Bath Chronicle*, Sam Holliday, has kindly given permission to use them.

The Museum of Bath at Work proved to be a treasure house of pictures. The Harbutt Archive, owned by Steve Lord, is held there, and we had permission from him to use photographs from it. The museum also holds a set of slides taken by Ian Ollis in the 1970s and 1980s, which provided some astonishing colour pictures of the restoration years. I would like to thank Stuart Burroughs, Director of the Museum of Bath at Work, for drawing my attention to these.

Colin Baker has allowed me to use his photograph of the Ladydown aqueduct, which he obtained while working for Network Rail. As far as I am aware, this is the only picture of the aqueduct in the public realm. The Bath Royal Literary and Scientific Institute gave permission for me to use their picture of the Somersetshire Coal Wharf. At a late stage, Susan Tully produced a photograph of the buildings on Widcombe Wharf, which had been owned by her father. Finally, we are very grateful to Bath artist Nick Cudworth for allowing us to use the pastel of the bridge in Sydney Gardens on the front cover and as a frontispiece. Prints of this can be obtained from his gallery at 5 London Street, Bath (www.nickcudworth.co.uk).

Detailed picture credits are as follows:
Colin Baker: 83 (left);
Robert Coles: 122, 166 (bottom right);
Gordon Collier: 178, 179 (both);

Bruce Crofts: 107, 111 (bottom), 112 (right), 114 (top right, bottom right);
Nick Cudworth: i;
Paul De'Ath: 86 (top), 88 (top right), 93 (bottom left), 94 (bottom right), 95 (bottom), 97 (top), 100 (top left), 102 (left, top right), 104 (bottom right), 105 (both), 111 (top), 114 (top left, bottom left), 115 (top left), 117 (top right, bottom right), 118 (centre), 119 (top left), 120 (top left), 128 (bottom left), 131 (top), 132 (top right), 133 (left), 135, 136 (top, bottom right)), 137, 138, 139, 140 (top), 141 (top, bottom), 142-3 (all), 144 (top left), 145 (top right), 146 (top right), 164 (bottom right), 166 (bottom left), 168, 184 (both), 189 (top left, top right);
Lizzy Doe: vi;
James Fagan: 189 (bottom left, bottom right), 190, 192 (bottom right), 193;
Jean Fry: 103, 128 (top right);
Geoffrey Hiscocks: 132 (top left);
The Knill Family: 101 (bottom right);
Dennis Lanham: 131 (bottom), 132 (bottom left);
Steve Lord: 101 (top right), 102 (bottom right), 104 (top right), 182;
Ian Ollis (Museum of Bath at Work): vii, xii, 7, 15, 16, 28 (bottom left), 31 (bottom left, bottom right), 34 (bottom left), 43 (top left), 49 (bottom right), 62 (top right), 64 (top), 67 (top left), 72 (top right), 80 (bottom right), 85 top right), 87, 88 (top left, bottom left), 90 (bottom right), 96 (bottom), 97 (bottom), 98 (top right), 99, 100 (bottom left), 101 (bottom left), 106 (right), 116 (top), 120 (top right, bottom right), 121 (bottom left, top right, centre right, bottom right), 123 (bottom), 124 (bottom left), 125 (top left, top centre), 125 (top right), 160 (top left), 185 (bottom right), 186-7 (all), 191;
Sue Tully: 119 (top right).

Bibliography

Books and articles about the Kennet & Avon Canal

Kennet & Avon Canal Trust, *Crofton Pumping Station Guide*

Kennet & Avon Canal Trust, *The Butty*, various issues

Allsop, Niall, *The Kennet & Avon Canal: A User's Guide*, Millstream Books, Bath, 1987

Berry, Warren, *The Kennet and Avon Navigation*, Phillimore, Chichester, 2009

Buchanan, Brenda J, 'The Avon Navigation and the Inland Port of Bath' in *Bath History VI*, Millstream Books, Bath, 1996

Clew, Kenneth R, *The Kennet & Avon Canal*, David & Charles, Newton Abbot, 2nd edition 1973

Clew, Kenneth R, *Wessex Waterway*, Moonraker Press, Bradford on Avon, 1978

Elliott, Kirsten, 'All About Eva' in *Archive: The Quarterly Journal for British Industrial and Transport History*, 27, Lightmoor Press, Lydney, 2000

Jones, Peter Lindley, *Restoring the Kennet & Avon Canal*, Tempus, Stroud, 2002

Penruddocke, Charles, 'On the Kennet & Avon Canal' in *Cosmopolitan*, 1888

Russell, John, *The Kennet & Avon Canal: A Journey from Newbury to Bath in 1964*, Millstream Books, Bath 1997

Smith, Cyril Herbert, *Through the Kennet & Avon Canal by Motorboat in 1928*, George Roberts, London, 1929

Other sources: Canals

Clew, Kenneth, *The Somersetshire Coal Canal and Railways*, David & Charles, Newton Abbot, 1970

Dalby, LJ, *The Wilts & Berks Canal*, Oakwood Press, Headington, Oxford, 2nd ed, 1986

Halse, Roger & Simon Castens, *The Somersetshire Coal Canal: A Pictorial Journey*, Millstream Books, Bath, 2000

Harris, Robert, *Canals and their Architecture*, Godfrey Cave Associates, London, 2nd ed, 1980

Smith, Donald J, *The Horse on the Cut*, Patrick Stevens, Cambridge, 1982

Somersetshire Coal Canal Society, *The Weigh House*, various issues

General

Bath & Country Graphic, various issues, 1897-1904

Bradby, Edward, *Seend: A Wiltshire Village Past and Present*, Alan Sutton, Gloucester, 2nd edition 1982

Buchanan, R Angus, 'The Bridges of Bath' in *Bath History III*, Alan Sutton, Gloucester, 1990

Mee, Arthur, *The King's England: Berkshire*, Hodder & Stoughton, London, 1939

Sims, Percy, *A History of Saltford Village*, PT Sims & RM Mawditt, Saltford, 1976

Swift, Andrew & Kirsten Elliott, *Bath Pubs*, Akeman Press, Bath, 2003

Swift, Andrew & Kirsten Elliott, *The Lost Pubs of Bath*, Akeman Press, Bath, 2005

Various contributors, *Bathwick: A Forgotten Village*, Bathwick Local History Society, Bath, 2004

Various contributors, *Bathwick: Echoes of the Past*, Bathwick Local History Society, Bath, 2008

White, Elizabeth (ed), *Keynsham & Saltford, Life and Work in Times Past 1539 – 1945*, Keynsham & Saltford Local History Society, 1990

Malpass, Peter & Andy King, *Bristol's Floating Harbour: The First 200 Years*, Redcliffe Press, Bristol, 2009

Websites

I have used various local history websites, but in particular the Kennet & Avon Trust website at www.katrust.org. This useful source gives details of Trust boats, as well as some of the historic details I was unable to find in other books.

1. Queen of Waters (Nancy Kerr)

Well away my love away
For we're sailing home today
On a boat called memory
Hail home, hearts that long for the land

Oh she's like some Persian queen
With her opal robes serene
In the lamplight shimmering
Hail home, hearts that long for the land

On a blue-jay morning
Feathering thorny memories
Hail home, hearts have been too long away
On a well-worn byway travelling
Magpie gathering
Farewell queen of waters

Well it's hard to roll in mirth
When your feet don't touch the earth
And the wolf comes hungering
Hail home, hearts that long for the land

Folly never foots the bill
And we all shall pay in full
For a life of melody
Hail home, hearts that long for the land

Well I should have sowed my corn
But I danced until the dawn
Like an ant grasshoppering
Hail home, hearts that long for the land

Oh there must be better ways
For to keep the debts at bay
And the whiskey trickling
Hail home, hearts that long for the land

So we'll bid our ship adieu
There's a mooring in the blue
Where the gulls are gathering
Hail home, hearts that long for the land

Oh she's like some Persian queen
And her like shall ne'er be seen
Only in our reverie
Hail home, hearts that long for the land

NAVIGATOR041

A farewell to the Kennet and Avon Canal.

AT WILCOT